David Mamet

A COLLECTION OF
Dramatic Sketches
and Monologues

SAMUEL FREN

45 WEST 25TH STREET
7623 SUNSET BOULEVARD
LONDON

HOLLYWOOD 90046
TORONTO

D1354312

ISBN 0 573 68908 3   Printed in U.S.A.

IMPORTANT BILLING AND CREDIT REQUIREMENTS

All producers of the pieces by David Mamet herein must give credit to the author in all programs distributed in connection with performances of the pieces and in all instances in which the titles of the pieces appear for the purpose of advertising, publicizing or otherwise exploiting the pieces and/or productions thereof. The name of the author must appear on a separate line, on which no other name appears, immediately following the title, and shall be in size of type at least 65% the size of title type.

TABLE OF CONTENTS

Two Conversations

Five Unrelated Pieces

Cast
(*in order of speaking*)

(Two Scenes — "One")

One .... Peter Maloney
Ann Spettell

(Two Conversations — "Two")

Two .... Peter Phillips
Jude Ciccolella

(Two Scenes — "Two")

Three.............................. Diane Venora

(Two Conversations — "One")

Four .... Dan Ziskie
James Rebhorn
Deborah Hedwall
Melodie Somers

Yes, But So What.................... David Rasche
Frank Girardeau

Stage Manager .... Lisa Difranza
Assistant to the Director.............. Robin Bowers

This play was produced in April 1983 at the Ensemble
Studio Theatre, Curt Dempster, Artistic Director, David
S. Rosenak, Managing Director.

Two Conversations

After dinner conversation. A and B, two women. C and
*   D, two men.*

C. (*hands D a note*) Read it.
D. "I can't come today be . . ."
A. Who is this?
C. That's our house . . .
D. It's the house cleaner . . .
C. Read it.
D. "I can't come today because something has hap-
pened to me." Is this the. . . ?
C. Yes.
D. Last week. . . ?
C. Yes.
D. He . . . he came, he came, didn't . . .
C. He came to leave the note.
D. I'd . . . do you mind if I tell . . .
A. You two have the same. . . ?
C. We gave him to them. He . . .
D. He was a wonderful . . .
C. You've seen him here.
A. No. I don't . . .
B. What does he look like?
D. Thirty-five. Small, thin, balding . . .
D. This man does such fantastic work . . .
B. What hap. . . ?
C. *Apparently* . . . well, tell them about . . .
D. I got a phone call. (*pause*) I was at the office, I
was between . . . this was, when. . . ?
C. Last . . .
D. Last *Monday*. He'd been at my house Sat . . .

7

C. He . . . yes. Yes. Saturday.

D. Monday I get a call. "I have to confess something. I have something important to talk . . ."

A. Had you talked be . . .

D. We'd never been, no. No. He'd never . . . "How are *you*?" The *weather* . . . so on. *So:*

C. . . . this happened to him, too, four years ago. When he . . .

D. When he first came to . . .

A. . . . where did he. . . ?

D. Up . . .

C. . . . when he . . .

D. Upstate.

C. When he, yes. When he first started with . . . I had to call his father. He came in . . .

A. This . . .

D. Yes.

A. This is four *years* ago . . .

D. Yes.

C. . . . He came in one day. I came in. (*pause*) He was sitting on the floor. His *shirt* was off. He was just sitting there. He'd been there a—1 day. And he saw nothing unusu . . .

D. That's the *thing* . . . that's the *thing* . . . that's the *point* . . . that's what I always say. As . . . wait. As *crazy* . . . as *unhappy* as we think we are, the line between psychotic and neurotic is not a thin line. (*pause*) It's not a thin divider at all. It's like. I think it's like . . . It's like the difference between . . . (*pause*) It's, um, like the difference between competence and talent. (*pause*)

A. What do you think causes . . .

D. . . . between . . .

A. What do you think causes it?

D. Psy. . . ? I . . . I don't know. *Genetic* . . . Um. (*a pause*) *Diet* . . .

C. An imbalance of some kind . . .

D. Yes. An imbalance. Yes. That isn't pred . . .

B. He worked for both of you. . . ?

D. That isn't predicated . . .

C. Yes . . .

D. On some mistaken *notion*. Do you know what I mean?

C. That's much *deeper* . . .

A. People living in their own dream don't know that they're in a dream. (*pause*)

C. Absolutely.

D. *Um. Now*: an example: if you were *unhappy* you could *say* so. You'd say "God, I hate myself". Or . . .

A. Mm Hmm . . .

D. "God, I'm fat . . ."

A. Mm hmm . . .

D. *He* doesn't *know* that. He is in a *dream*.

A. He'd been committed before?

D. Yes.

C. When he first worked for us.

B. Um hm.

C. Tell them last week.

D. Last week: last *Monday*, he called me at work "I have to talk to you." Did you see . . . what *was* that . . .?

C. Some *German* picture . . .

D. Some *German* thing. Where the same thing happened . . .

C. . . . I don't know the name of it . . .

D. He'd stolen two decks of cards. (*pause*) He called me. But I couldn't talk. "I have to talk to you. I have to confess. I've taken your cards."

C. . . . he asked *me* . . .

D. Yes . . .

C. I said "Don't call. You see/ You're putting him in an . . ."

D. It was a cry for *help*.

A. *Certainly*.

C. " . . . in an embarrassing . . ."

D. I mean the *cards* were worth, what? Two dollars . . .

C. In an embarrassing position. Yes. It was a . . .

D. Well, that's what I *told* him that was the

A. . . . the only way he had . . .

D. Yes.

C. I told him to for . . .

D. He told him to forget it. Then he called *Me*. Then *Jim* called. I told him . . .

C. Wait. Tell them about the A . . .

D. Oh yes. He says "Did you. . . ?"

C. . . . that *German* film . . .

D. "Did you see the . . . "um . . . um . . . "No, why. . . ?" "Because your *ace* is missing." (*pause*)

A. That was in some film?

D. Yes. It signified . . . I don't know . . .

C. "You're in danger", he says.

D. "Jim . . . Jim . . ."

C. I said it was just his way of at . . .

D. Of attracting attention. *Certainly* . . .

B. *Wait*. (*pause*) he took *playing* cards? (*pause*)

D. Yes. (*pause*)

B. *Why*? (*pause*) Why, do you think? (*pause*)

D. I don't know.

B. *Because* of the movie. (*pause*)

A. What do you mean?

B. So he could take the ace and say he had a, you know . . . (*pause*)

D. A reason to call *up*.

B. Yes. (*pause*)

D. Hm. Well. You may be right.

C. When this happened before he was in for six months. When he came *out* . . .

D. He did such a marvellous job . . .

C. This house was *spotless*. There was nothing you would not *eat* off of. Seriously . . .

D. He treated it as an art.

C. He *did*. Yes. That's exactly how he treated it.

D. He treated it as an art, he was *inventive*.

C. . . . yes.

D. . . . he was . . .

C. . . . he . . .

D. . . . he was *dependable* . . .

C. When he got out he *came* to me and asked me would I try him again. Which of course I *did* . . .

A. And he was fine?

C. Yes.

A. Mm.

C. Fade out, fade in . . .

D. Four years later.

C. Mm.

D. So: when he *called* I said:

C. He said to call *me*.

D. I couldn't talk to him . . .

C. Waal, it couldn't have helped in any case. (*pause*) He . . .

A. He didn't want to *confess* . . . He

D. He wanted to be helped. Yes.

C. He . . . he *came* to me. He said, "I need a rest." I said, "*Jim*. You don't need a rest. You need serious help." (*pause*)

B. I'm sure that he felt incredibly lonely, or he would never have done what he did. (*pause*) I know I would feel very lonely if that happened to *me*. (*pause*)

C. *Well*. (*pause*) He asked me to call his father . . .

D. The fellow, all his friends, he picks them up at four a.m. on the streets . . .

C. . . .and so I *did*, and he . . .

D. . . . . this is the interesting part:

C. He says "He's no good. He never was any good. He's a bum. He always . . ."

D. This, this is his father talking . . .

C. "And he always was. He never should have come down to New *York*. Since he *got* there he . . ."

D. *Mmm. . ./*?

C. "He's done *nothing*? I said. "Sir. Your son has a thriving *business*. On the *contrary*: he's . . . I've seen his *accounts*. He's *organized* (*pause*) He's *meticulous* . . . he does his job *superlatively* . . . (*pause*) He's *reliable* . . . he's *not* a bum. He's *Ill.* (*pause*) He's *ill.* He needs *help*. (*pause*)

A. Did the father come down?

C. *No*. We took him to . . .

D. We took him to Bellevue. (*pause*)

A. Will they take good care of him there?

D. Yes. I think they will. Yes.

C. Yes. They will. (*pause*)

A. Do you think that's treatable?

C. Yes. I think that it is. Yes. And I don't. I'll tell you something, I don't think its in the *mind*, either . . .

B. What?

C. Schizophrenia.

A. Schiz . . .

C. No. I think it's cau . . .

A. It isn't in the *mind*. . . ?

C. I'm saying that its *cause* . . . I think the *cause* is not. (*pause*) That the true *cause* of it is not *trauma* . . . or . . . Infantile *trauma* or . . . say what I'm saying . . .

D. That the cause is something simple. *Die* or genetic . . .

C. *Yes.*

D. Genetic pre . . .

A. Predisposition.

D. Yes.

C. And I'll tell you what *else*: I think *someday some-one's* going to find how to *cure* schizophrenia with a . . . say with a simple *touch* . . . with . . . (*pause*) with a small change in *diet* . . . (*a pause*) with . . .

D. Mm hmm . . .

C. . . . with a *pressure* point . . . with . . .

D. . . . with a simple *touch*. (*pause*)

C. Yes. (*pause*) Absolutely. (*pause*)

A. Will he be in there long?

C. I don't know.

A. Will you take him back when he comes out?

C. Certainly.

D. Absolutely.

C. Absolutely. (*pause*)

END OF ONE

SCENE 2

After dinner conversation. A and B, two men.

A. . . . the way *I* understand it . . . the way *I* understand it . . . *I'll* tell you what the *Antichrist* is . . .

B. What?

A. I'll tell you, and I believe it will come. Although I *don't* believe we've seen it yet. When we'll *see it*, when we'll *see* it is in the *hard* . . . in the *true* . . . eh? In the *true true* hard times. And what I think the *antichrist* is is, the way that we can understand it's if we say "The False Girlfriend". (*pause*) Mm. When one is ready to be *married*. Then you say that *this* one has something *unique* which until now you *longed* for but . . .

B. . . . yes . . .

A. But you couldn't *find*. So now you've *found* it, now you can . . .

B. Um hmm . . .

A. Get *married*. (*pause*)

B. So now you can get married.

A. But it's just the *time* is right. That's all. The time is right; and *when* it is you *see* some one and say "She is the One". Now: Full of our old habits, the person that we see *first*—like a *policeman*. He sees the streets differently from a *cab* driver . . . they both see different things—so when we're *ready* . . .

B. Mm . . .

A. To *wed*—it could be our old *habits* cause our *sight* to fasten on . . .

B. Uh huh . . .

A. A . . .

B. . . . the false . . .

A. No. Not necessarily *false*. *Yes*. False. In a way. In that all that's *wrong*, finally, is that she . . . she's not the right—put in her place as, simply, as a "*woman*", *fine*. But as the girl for *you*, no. No. To *marry*? No. Because you're caught in your "pre-courtship . . ." No. "pre-*marriage* courtship context". Your *sight* . . . (*pause*) Your body says "wed". But your *soul*, your, no, your *habit's* still in that outmoded mode of *thinking*. So she's wrong. She's the wrong one. Although the *time* is right. You break up with this person. You find some one *new*. You *marry* and You say "Now how *extraordinary* that I found *two* such . . ."

B. . . . yes . . .

A. . . . and, if you *think*, you reason back and you see that it was only the *time* was right. Just like a *flower*.

(*pause*) That's all. So, with the *Antichrist* . . . it's just an
. . . here's where I think the New Test. It's . . .

B. . . . the New Testament . . .

A. . . . it's *brilliant*. What it *is* is, finally, I think, I
could be wrong, perhaps not in *entirety*, but perhaps *so*;
I don't know. What it is is allegory for *marriage*. (*pause*)
The *Christ*, the *antichrist* . . . *reunion* . . .

B. You're saying it's pri . . .

A. What?

B. It's primarily a ho . . .

A. A what?

B. A homosexual relationship.

A. What is?

B. I don't mean a ho . . . I mean a homosexual *romance* . . .

A. No. (*pause*) *Perhaps* it is. (*pause*) No. Because
we're . . . Ah. Because we're waiting for that *man* . . .

B. For that one man . . .

A. No, perhaps so, huh. (*pause*) Huh. (*pause*) What
are you saying? (*pause*)

B. That it's a homosexual romance.

A. Huh. (*pause*)

B. No. I'm not saying that. I'm asking if . . .

A. If *I* implied that.

B. Yes.

A. If the New Testament . . . (*pause*) No. I don't
think so. (*pause*) You're . . . wait a second. I said it's
an . . .

B. . . . it's an allegory . . .

A. . . . it's an allegory for . . .

B. . . . mmm hmm . . .

A. But what *you're* saying . . .

B. Yes. For marriage. But it's not a reconciliation
with the . . .

A. With the *Earth* . . .

B. Yes.

A. With the, um, um, with the *mother* figure . . . no.

B. But . . .

A. Yes. Mmm. With the . . . yes . . .

B. Yes. With the . . .

A. But with the *father*. (*pause*)

B. It's not a hetero . . .

A. No . . .

B. If we . . .

A. Yes. Taken as a romance. No. (*pause*) Mm. Striving for . . . (*pause*) No. (*pause*) Wait a second. (*pause*) Now: what are we: what are we . . . what are we *saying* here: Let's step back . . . (*pause*) That christianity is . . . (*pause*) I started off, I said that the *antichrist* is The False Girlfriend . . .

B. Is *like* the false . . .

A. But it would be the false *Boyfriend* is what you're saying. (*pause*) You're saying that the whole religion's basically an apology for homosexuality.

B. I don't think that I'm saying that.

A. Well. It's the logical extension of your . . . A reunion with the *Father*. A refusal to accept the . . . um . . . the weight of. Hetero . . . *essentially* . . . wait . . . wait a second: *mate*, have *children*, *bequeath* . . . the *seed* bank . . . pass on your, um, and *die*. Essentially the hetero . . . and what *you're* saying . . . well. Well, You. Um. And living *forever*. (*pause*) That You will Live Forever. It's a, yes, it's basically a refusal to *change*. *Continence* . . . um, we are assured that if we plight our troth to the *father* figure we will not d . . . which is, um, to say we will not grow *up*. We will not grow *old*. Ha. So we have discovered the . . . wait, we have discovered the Perfect Man. We fall in love with him, and we will not grow old. Yes. It's a homosexual romance. Yes. If we, what? If we *sufficiently*, if we love him with all our *hearts* (*pause*) Um. (*pause*) It really has nothing to do with *women, does it*? (*pause*) No. (*pause*) mmm. (*pause*) And his attachment to his *mother*! Well, no, not *his*, but *ours* . . . um . . . we can't . . . we can't *divorce* ourselves from . . . Oh! Oh! Oh! and the Weak, Absent *Father*! Hm! The Father Cuckholded! The impotent . . . the failure of the marriage . . . Ha! Ha! (*pause*) Ha! (*pause*) Ha! Oh! Oh! I've got to . . . (*gets up*) excuse me . . .

    B. Will I see you. . . ?

    A. Yes. I'll call you tonight.

END OF TWO

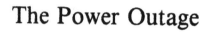

The Power Outage

The Power Outage

1. The thing which I'm telling you is no one enjoys being equal.

2. Yes. Yes. I agree with that. We have our fictions. And what did you do when the lights went out?

1. Stumbled around in the dark. (*sotto voce*) . . . taking goods away . . . they took the goods away. (*full voice*) Goods cannot take away heat.

2. No.

1. As if, if they were stolen, they could take the dark away.

2. No. I agree with you.

1. A flashlight runs on batteries, as does a candle, if you follow me.

2. (*sotto voce*) No.

1. But here we find electric light has a connection.

2. Yes. I see your point. Yes.

1. Like a road, eh?

2. Yes.

1. It is the same road. One for all. A dirt path in the Hinterlands, or some worn blacktop in the Ozarks. It is all the same. One road.

2. (*sotto voce*) One road.

1. Now we see the same of electricity. Why do we need these things?

2. The goods?

1. Yes. (*pause*)

2. They keep us cool.

1. Oh. (*sighs*) I tell you. It's like being at the Y.

2. The Blackout?

1. Yes. When you have taken off your clothes and they cannot see where you bought your watch.

2. (*sotto voce*) Mmm.

1. When they turned the power off. So when the men were in the streets all bets were off.

2. (*sotto voce*) When they went after goods. I know. It says they put them forty to a room too small for ten.

1. They did?

2. I read they did.

1. When they had caught them.

2. Yes.

1. You know, when you go in a record store you see the men with guns.

2. I know.

1. In Medieval England we learn they had seven hundred crimes which they could hang you for. We see that, and we are aghast. But now, today, you see them in the Supermarkets with their guns. They are empowered to kill you for the theft of record albums. (*pause*) Of some diversionary device or machine.

2. (*to self*) And they were very hot in there.

1. So when the men were in the streets, they said all bets are off. "You cannot live in Darkness. You insure your power by the gun." (*pause*) What audacity.

2. I think so, too.

1. Today you cannot buy a flashlight.

2. It is difficult, but you can buy them.

1. Do you know, the folks directing traffic . . .

2. Yes.

1. Controlling traffic in their nightdress, as in Revolutionary Times. This is not altruism.

2. No. We'd all like to direct it.

1. It is wish-fulfillment.

2. (*to self*) Until they came to Trial . . .

1. Or they would go destroy a mercantile concern.

2. (*to self, continuing*) which would not be soon . . .

1. And cause much unhappiness. (*pause*)

2. Someone should write a book.

1. There. In the dark. Our dreams of courage, or The Indians. Of foraging.

2. We all revert.

1. You think so?

2. Yes.

The Dog

CAST

MAN . . . . John Savoia

Directed by . . . . Joe Cacaci

The Dog

MAN. Talk about a dog! Talk about a precious animal! A little fluffball. A furry little nothing. But ballsy as a paratrooper.

He's tough but I'm tougher. Bengy may be high but I'm yet tougher.

Go after dogs twice his size. Three, four times his size. Go right up to 'em Sniff 'em. Smell 'em up and down . . .

He growls, bares his teeth.

He scares 'em. He's little, but goddamn it if he's not a scrapper. And they know it. Damn right they do, too.

Sensitive?

He's more sensitive than most *people*. Makes most people look sick, he's so sensitive. In tune like a human.

He picks up on things, too.

I come home, he meets me at the door. Grinning, breathing fast, he's glad to see me.

I go to hang up my coat, and what do I find? The little pisser has shit on the floor! – He's crossed me. My best friend has crossed me.

So I go over to him. He's grinning like a sonofabitch, and I say *sit*. And he sits down and cocks his head, wondering what's up.

I make a fist, and lean over and whack the shit outta him. He goes clear across the room and just lays there on his side.

So then I say *get up* and he gets up. And I say *sit* and he sits down again and I walk over to him.

So he's purebred, he's no dummy. And he figures maybe I'm going to knock him around again, and he's a little scared.

27

But he hangs right in there.

I say *stay*. And it's like he's glued to the floor. He'd sit there for a year if I didn't tell him different.

So I go over and get a chair and bring it back and put it right in front of him. I sit down, lean back, and cross my legs.

I look at him. He looks at me.

After a minute or so, I lean forward and say, very reasonable and soft, I say "Don't shit on the floor". "Now, get outta here".

And I never have to say a word on the subject again.

Film Crew

CAST

MIKE..................................Brian Smiar
JOE ....John Savoia

Directed by ....Joe Cacaci

Film Crew

Two Men

JOE. Did you make this up?

MIKE. No. I mean, you know, I *embellished* it. Yeah. I made part of it up.

JOE. Uh huh.

MIKE. The nice thing, you know, I guess I've taught it to, say ten or fifteen crews . . .

JOE. Uh huh.

MIKE. . . . over the last four years, the *nice* thing, I'll be out somewhere, some one will say "I'll teach you this . . .", and I can trace it back. "Where did you *learn* it from. . . ?", and I can trace it back to, you know . . .

JOE. Yeah . . .

MIKE. To someone who I taught. (*pause*) And, you know, you play *tournaments* . . . and you can play for *money* . . .

JOE. How?

MIKE. You play *points.*

JOE. Oh. Yeah.

MIKE. Sure. And what you have left in your hand is what you're stuck with.

JOE. Whoever goes *out.*

MIKE. Yeah. If you're stuck with fifteen *points* . . .

JOE. Uh huh . . .

MIKE. and you can play, you know, a *dime* a point, *penny* a point . . .

JOE. . . . yeah.

MIKE. . . . *buck* a point. You get stuck with an *ace* in your hand, that's fifteen bucks right there.

JOE. Right.

MIKE. One night on my last shoot. . . ?

JOE. Uh huh?

MIKE. Night shoot?

JOE. Yeah?

MIKE. To get to sleep, we musta played, six, seven games. (*pause*) We were up, jesus, til noon. I won a hundren twenty bucks.

JOE. Yeah?

MIKE. *Oh* yeah. Oh yeah. *Easily.* (*pause*)

JOE. Now, what's this thing with Jacks?

MIKE. It's simple: If you play a Jack, then you must cover it. (*pause*)

JOE. Uh huh.

MIKE. With another card. (*pause*)

JOE. "Cover" it. (*pause*)

MIKE. Play another card on top of it.

JOE. Right.

MIKE. Of the same suit.

JOE. Right.

MIKE. Or denomination.

JOE. Right. And it you can't?

MIKE. You have to draw another card. *But!* But, of course, if you have more than one Jack in your hand, then you can play *that* Jack on it. (*pause*)

JOE. Uh huh.

MIKE. So, you'd play your Jack, you have to *cover* it. (*pause*) Are you with me?

JOE. Yes.

MIKE. Alright. You cover it with another Jack. And then you have to cover it again.

JOE. Again?

MIKE. Of course. Because you've played a Jack.

JOE. Right. Alright.

MIKE. You see?

JOE. Yes.

MIKE. It's still a Jack.

JOE. Yes. Right.

MIKE. And you can play as many Jacks as you've got in your hand, with, of course, with two decks, that's eight Jacks. If you have them in your hand.

JOE. And you cover the last card.

MIKE. Yes. Now. Now: For each Jack you play, you skip one man. (*pause*)

JOE. Uh huh.

MIKE. So: you play your Jack, you skip the man to your ri left; second Jack, two, men. et cetera.

JOE. Right.

MIKE. It's simple.

JOE. And the last card that you cover must be the same suit.

MIKE. Right. Just like any other card. (*pause*) Or denomination.

JOE. Right. Except that that would be a Jack.

MIKE. Right. Right. I'm sorry. Or an eight. (*pause*)

JOE. What's this thing with fours?

MIKE. Fours. Very simple. When you play a *four* . . . when you play a *four* . . . ?

JOE. Yes?

MIKE. The direction of play changes. (*pause*) Right?

JOE. Right. (*pause*)

MIKE. It's very simple: man on your right plays, *you* play. You play a four, it goes right back to him. Now *he* must play again. (*pause*) You see?

JOE. Yes. And then the man on *his* right.

MIKE. Yes. (*pause*) You must changed the *direction*.

JOE. Right.

MIKE. Good. (*pause*) That's it. Other than that it's regular.

JOE. How do you score?

MIKE. Aces are *fifteen* . . .

JOE. . . . yes . . .

MIKE. Face cards are *ten* . . .

JOE. Uh huh.

MIKE. And every other thing is what it is. (*pause*) Okay?

JOE. Yes.

MIKE. Wait. (*pause*) You know about the Queen of Spades?

JOE. No.

MIKE. Queen of Spades, the next man takes five cards. (*pause*) If you play the Queen of Spades the next man must take five cards.

JOE. From the stack.

MIKE. Yes. (*pause*) *Unless* he plays the Queen of Spades right back at you.

JOE. Can he do that?

MIKE. Of course. There's two, right?

JOE. Right.

MIKE. And that's the game. You want to try a practice hand? Wait! Wait: this is an important rule. Now: When you have . . . wait. When you've played all of your cards but one *card* . . . huh?

JOE. . . . yes?

MIKE. When you have only one card left to play, then you say "Last Card".

JOE. "Last Card".

MIKE. You must announce: "Last Card". If you *fail* you must take ten cards from the stack. (*pause*) You must say "Last Card" *before* the next man on your left plays. Or wherever. Before the next man plays. This is important, because *sometimes* you'll have one card and you'll forget to announce, so there's two guys on the far side, right, sitting over here, and you can call it any time until the next man plays, and *save* yourself, so we're here waiting for the next guy to *play*, right? And you can call it any time. So we're avoiding your *eyes* . . .

JOE. Right . . .

MIKE. And trying not to call *attention* . . . so that he will play, and we can call it on you. Before you remember. (*pause*) Ha.

JOE. Does that happen very often?

MIKE. Oh. Oftener than you might think. *Oh* yeah.

JOE. Mm.

MIKE. *Oh* yeah. (*pause*) And that's the game. (*pause*) That's it. Do you want to try a practice hand?

Four A.M.

CAST

GREG.............................Bill Cwikowski
CALLER ....Michael Wikes

Directed by ....Joe Cacaci

Four A.M.

An announcer seated at a radio studio console desk. He wears earphones and speaks into a microphone. We hear the voice of the CALLER over a loudspeaker.

INTERVIEWER. Hello, you're on the air.

CALLER. Hello, Greg, how are you?

INTERVIEWER. I'm fine.

CALLER. Good. Greg, it's a pleasure to talk with you. I've had the pleasure of talking to you three and one half *years* ago, and I've been a continual listener of yours since you started out with the twenty-two stations, and I admire you very much.

INTERVIEWER. Thank you.

CALLER. Thank *you*, Greg.

INTERVIEWER. What's your problem?

CALLER. Greg, we need your help to publicise our plan. We've been trying to get our organization together to raise money to be able to hire a public relations firm like Wells and Jacoby to publicise our organization. (*pause*) Where are we going to *get* the money. . . ? *I* don't know . . .

INTERVIEWER. To publicise your . . .

CALLER. In the movie *Two Thousand and One*, based on the writings of Arnold Toynbee, they speak of the plan . . .

INTERVIEWER. Excuse me, excuse me, but the movie *Two Thousand and One* was based on the writings . . .

CALLER. . . . . all human life is made of molecules . . .

INTERVIEWER. . . . . based on the writings of Arthur C. Clarke . . .

CALLER. All human . . . no, Greg, if you examine . . .

INTERVIEWER. . . . . it was based on the writings of Arthur C. Clarke . . .

39

CALLER. Oh, Greg, *No.* We have the . . .

INTERVIEWER. Well, go on.

CALLER. . . . we have the writings.

INTERVIEWER. Okay, go on.

CALLER. *Greg:* In the writings of Arnold Toynbee he discusses a plan whereby all human life could be easily reconstituted on the planet Jupiter.

INTERVIEWER. Uh huh . . . (*pause*)

CALLER. Greg?

INTERVIEWER. Yes? (*pause*) I'm listening.

CALLER. Greg . . .

INTERVIEWER. Yes?

CALLER. In the wr . . .

INTERVIEWER. Yeah. I got it. Go on.

CALLER. In the . . .

INTERVIEWER. No, no. no. Go *on.* I *got* it. Arnold Toynbee, human life on . . .

CALLER. As we're made of molecules, Greg and the *atoms* of all human life that ever lived are still in all of us . . .

INTERVIEWER. Okay, I got it. They exist, they've just been rearranged. (*pause*)

CALLER. Yes. (*pause*)

INTERVIEWER. *So?*

CALLER. We'd like to publicise our organization, Greg. We're very young. We've just been in existence over a year and we want to *publicise* our theory. And, Greg, we don't know *how.*

INTERVIEWER. You . . . how do you publicise your plan to bring dead people back to life on *Jupiter.*

CALLER. Yes.

INTERVIEWER. *Why*? (*pause*) Why would you want to do this? (*pause*) Hello?

CALLER. Yes?

INTERVIEWER. Why would you want to *do* this? (*pause*) You see what I'm saying to you? (*pause*) What is the aim of your group?

CALLER. *Greg* . . .

INTERVIEWER. What are your *plans*? (*pause*)

CALLER. I . . . (*pause*)

INTERVIEWER. *What*?

CALLER. I . . . Greg, I *told* you.

INTERVIEWER. You said that you want to bring dead people back to life.

CALLER. Yes.

INTERVIEWER. On the planet Jupiter.

CALLER. Just as they showed us in the mo . . .

INTERVIEWER. Well, I'm not sure that's what the movie was about, but be that as it may, why would you want to do that?

CALLER. Oh, Greg, you can't *mean* it . . .

INTERVIEWER. Well, *yes*, I mean it. Why would you . . . what's the idea. . . ? You're walking down the street, there's Abraham *Lincoln* . . . is that the idea?

CALLER. Yes.

INTERVIEWER. . . . so anybody that you want to *talk* to, so forth, there they are. Is that the idea? (*pause*)

CALLER. Yes.

INTERVIEWER. Who do you *pick*? Who *pick's* 'em? You? Your organization? . . . or do you just bring 'em *all* back? (*pause*) What is your . . . I mean, do you have a *program* for this? Or . . . what are your *goals*. . . . ? (*pause*)

CALLER. To bring . . .

INTERVIEWER. Naah . . . it's too *broad*. It's too *broad*. Don't you see what I'm talking about? You can't bring 'em *all* back. (*pause*) *Can* you?

CALLER. I don't know.

INTERVIEWER. Well, *think* about it. (*pause*) *Think* about it. You're talking about billions of people. Eh? They've *lived* at different times. They speak different *languages*—the ones that speak our language, it's *changed* over the years. The *dialects* are different. *Customs* change. Their *lives* are different. Some of them died violent *deaths* . . . some are *disfigured* . . . they've been *decomposing* . . . Now: listen to this: at what point do you bring them *back*? (*pause*) Right before they *died*? What if they were *ill*? What if they were *infirm*? And so you don't do it then, when *do* you do it? At what point? You see what I'm telling you? Someone wants to come back at age *twenty*, so you bring him back at fifty-five . . . is he allowed to *change*? And who's to say if he can or he can't? What if he never wanted to come back?

CALLER. . . . Greg. . . ?

INTERVIEWER. What about people who *killed* themselves. Because they didn't want to live? Some of them we know. We could leave *out*. What about ones that we *don't* know? Who's going to pass on this? You and your *group*? Well, then you're talking about something very much like fascism. Is this what you want? Because I'll tell you what you get very quickly is a State where only the *Pure* can come back. Or the good*looking* . . . or whatever the people in charge that day seem to feel is the ultimate good . . . and ticks their fancy. Or do you just press a button and *every*one comes back. And what do you have then? I'll *tell* you what you have: *wars*. You've got wars. Unless you think that being dead *improved* them. You see what I'm saying? You've got the same *jealousies* and misunder*stand*ings you had the *first* time. And how do you explain the technology to some guy who's just come back from 1565 and all of a sudden he's in some *space* suit and he's *alive* again . . .

CALLER. He wouldn't be in a space suit.

INTERVIEWER. . . .whatever. And who *governs* this august group? Or do they just 'get along'? Not in *this* lifetime, friend. What do you think? because they're on a foreign planet that it's going to be co-operation and good *will*? They're going to forget about their human nature and just live in joy? You're talking about *heaven*, my friend. Heaven doesn't exist. You think the fact that they've come back is going to make them all philosophers? I don't think so. For a *day, yes. MAYbe*. A week, a month later, and I'm going to tell you something: it's going to be worse than it was before, and you know what you've got? Chaos. And any time you get a *State* like that you have a populace that thinks the world owes it a living. And you've got a tragedy. It doesn't hold up. Even as a dream. It's not thought-out. And what do they eat?

CALLER. Toynbee says we can bombard the atmosphere with oxygen and reclaim the soil.

INTERVIEWER. *Does* he? And what if he's *wrong. . .* ? (*pause*) You see what I'm saying? (*pause*)

CALLER. I . . .

INTERVIEWER. You see what I'm telling you?

CALLER. I . . .

INTERVIEWER. Listen to me. The world is full of histories of people trying to live in U*top*ias. It doesn't work. We wish it *did*, it *doesn't*. (*pause*) Alright? (*pause*) Alright?

CALLER. Um . . . yes.

INTERVIEWER. *Alright*. Thank you for calling. (*Loudspeaker goes dead.*) Let's move along:

Food

Food

Two Men

C. I've loved eating and I've *always* loved eating. My *father* died of insulin shock. The day they put him in the hospital his blood pressure was twenty over eighty, wanted to dose him with *insulin*, he told them "no". They *killed* him. They *killed* him. He, one time, had a saccharin reaction, in the 50's, when they took it, when it was in everything. He proved their case. (*pause*) He was the one, the cases of his type, why it's no longer in . . . in *sodas* . . . (*pause*) in *food* . . .

D. You're saying that it was his case?

C. Yes.

D. In what way, you're saying he took them to court?

C. Not in that sense, no. Cases of his type. You understand?

D. Yes.

C. (*pause*) And he overate. Those days . . . you know . . .

D. Yes.

C. You know how it was. *Later* we had no sugar in the house. You couldn't *find* it, for we didn't *have* it there. *Nothing*. And my mother was assiduous in cleansing it out; you remember, though when we were young. It was in *everything*. The *cereal* . . . the *tea* . . . the *coffee* . . . *rolls* . . . you could go right through the day . . . Lunch . . . (*pause*) My idea later on . . . dessert was half-a-grapefruit, but *then*, and you, too, I know. When we were young . . . the *oatmeal*. . ? My father put sugar on *fruit*.

D. My father, too?

C. My father put sugar on *water*melon.

D. My father did, too.

47

C. Looking back, he was a sick man. He was a very sick man. (*pause*) He must have been. All of the *effort* that he spent in balancing his diet; or, to say it on a different plane (because, finally, his diet did not admit of a balance): to achieve *rest*, he was trying to find *rest*. In himself. In food. For one moment. I think. In his life. Because of the *food* he ate. To overcome the *harm* that he had done, as I'm sure that he know. The *milk* to overcome the sugar; the *caffeine* to overcome the cloying effect of the milk, which, I think, in the future, will be seen to be the worst. The worst of what we eat, for *all* that we say it is natural.

D. What?

C. Dairy.

D. Dairy products.

C. Yes. And *nicotine* to calm the harm that he did with caffeine. And *meat* to give him energy he needed. Not for "life". Not for his daily "life", but to combat the effects of the *food*. He, I saw him put butter on his *steak* . . .

D. I've seen that, too.

C. And *salt*. (*pause*) Salt on everything. Sugar and salt. We put sugar on *straw*berries . . . (*pause*)

D. What about your mother? (*pause*)

C. She . . . my *mother* . . . (*pause*)

D. Yes.

C. As a *cook* . . .

D. Yes.

C. How was she as a *cook*. . . ?

D. Yes. (*pause*)

C. You know she died . . .

D. No. (*pause*)

C. She . . . she . . . (*pause*) She was the *cook*. (*pause*) She, uh, (*pause*) she cooked as she was *taught*. What else could she *do*? *Nothing.* What did *any* of us know? Nothing. "Eat Milk. It's Good for You!" And *alcohol.* Drink. . . ? (*pause*) He drank all night. That's how I was brought up. You, too. No—I won't *touch* it now.

D. You don't touch drink?

C. I'll tell you what else: I don't miss it. Not one bit. The hardest I think was caffeine. Aaaaaand *salt.* Well, it's in everything. I used to drink club *soda.* No. You can't drink that. It's *salt.* That's all it is. That's why they *drink* it. You can't lie to yourself. Because if you do your *body* will inform you. If you're lying to yourself. (*pause*) You see? (*pause*) As it starts to cleanse itself it will inform you. (*pause*) *Cigars.* You know me . . .

D. Yes.

C. Someone gave me one at *Thanksgiving* . . .

D. Mm.

C. An *Uppman.* I'd eaten too much. Eh? (*pause*) My body was *acid,* so I craved *nicotine.* And so I told myself. "Waaal, it's a *holiday,*" as if it were a reward to poison my system . . .

So I smoked the cigar . . . (*pause*) I didn't even *want* it. While I smoked it I had to remind myself that it was a reward. I woke up in the night in *sweat.* My sweat stank of cigars. The *sheets* stank. When I washed them they still smelled. Your body's a machine. As trite as it is it is true.

If you don't change it today when are you going to change it? (*pause*) *Never.* He died as he wouldn't change. He knew more than they knew. They killed him anyway. *Why*? Because he was helpless. Because he was *ill.* Then he was at their mercy. And, I want to tell you, any time that that occurs your opponents will harm you. That's the nature of the world. Not *me.* Not *me.* My body is my friend. It does not want to do me ill. It does not want to be diseased. It is my friend. (*pause*) It is not my enemy. It killed my father. It will not kill *me*. It killed my *brother*—it will not kill *me*. It has killed *many*. It will not kill *me*. It is my *friend*. My body is my *friend*.

Pint's a Pound
the World Around

CAST

A..W.H. Macy
B................................Joe Ponazecki

This play was first produced in May 1984 at the Ensemble Studio Theatre, Curt Dempster, Artistic Director, David S. Rosenak, Managing Director.

Pint's a Pound
the World Around

A. . . . don't have the twelve inch. We have the ten inch and the fourteen inch.

B. Isn't that always the way?

A. Seems it is. A number 2 do?

B. No.

A. Alright. The guys should have been in *Tuesday*, I spect him *Friday*, if he don't come then . . . I'll tell you, I've been thinking of switching. 'Merican *United*, I can get twenty percent over a year, you sign on to their Ownership Subscriber Plan, you get a basis of twenty percent, you want something it's *there*. The next day. Six days.

B. Where they out of?

A. Down in Manchester. *Basis* of twenty-percent, they've got a *newspaper*, what do you call it, a *flyer*, the *specials*, they can go, sometimes they beat the Market Way sixty percent.

B. No.

A. Absolutely.

B. How's the quality?

A. Same, better. Most things better, much of . . . what they *do*. *You* know, they've got their *brand* . . .

B. Uh huh . . .

A. *Good* stuff. Heavy gauge stuff. Some of . . . *you* know their stuff . . .

B. . . . sure . . .

A. . . . same patterns eighteen-ninety-eight . . .

B. When's that, when they got started?

A. When they got started. Yes. Fellow name of . . . I had the guy in here, I was looking at their stuff since I came in. You have to sign *up*, what you do, you buy stock in the *company*, the minimum buy-in thirty-two hundred dollars, you own *stock*, at the end of the year they go and pro*rate* you the amount of your sales, and you're discounted based on that.

B. And what do you do with the discount?

A. What do you do?

B. What, do you apply it to your . . .

A. Well, I guess you do. I never thought of it. I suppose that you . . . or you could take it in cash. I had the guy here just the other day.

B. They want you to sign up.

A. The closest, *Jims*, in *Brandenburgs* American . . .

B. He is. . . ?

A. Oh yeah. You see his prices in there? Beat the *Marketway* fifteen percent *easily*. On *everything*. He *has* to . . .

B. They spend their money on advertising.

A. That's what I'm *saying*. It ain't going in the *stock*, in stock improvement . . . dealer *relations* . . . it's going in the *television* ads. Schiff, started eighteen-ninety-eight. American United, the whole operation's built on one thing: the relation with the *dealer*.

B. Mm.

A. Stockholders are the dealer, *customers* the dealer. Everything. Geared toward one man. I pick up the phone, I say "Where are the . . . *whatever*, he said that they'd be here on *Thursday*." Marketway, what do *they* care. . . ? No *displays*, very few *incentives* . . . like I'm buying *retail* from them. You complain to someone, their attitude, basically, I think, I don't think they do it on *purpose*, but what you get is: if you don't want the franchise, you can turn back. They don't care. What they think, they're doing you a *favor*, all the money they've spent on the T.V. ads. Some stores, maybe, though I doubt it. Not in *here*.

A fella comes in here he wants three of those, four of those, something he broke on a job, he wants it this afternoon: *I'm* built on *service*. He goes down the road, he can go to the *Star* supply in *Worth*, he's in the habit to come here, I want to *keep* him here. Two things they told me: never change your hours, never cut your stock.

B. Uh huh.

A. A fellow comes by some hour you're spose to be open and you're *closed*, next time he thinks heavily fore he drives out of his way. "Maybe he's closed . . ."

B. That's very true.

A. . . . it makes no difference it only happened one time. It's like adultery. I'm not fooling you. He thinks "It happened once, it could happen again."

B. Uh huh.

A. Fellow comes in here, something he needs on a job, he needs it this afternoon. I'm *out* of it, what does he think? "*Shit*, I could of drove the same distance to *Star* and had it, and probably *cheaper* . . ." Something else. If I can get with the *American* I'm going to beat Marketway, I'm going to beat *Star* I'm going to have them coming *here* from Worth . . .

B. You think?

A. There's no two ways about it. I'll have the stock, I'll have the variety, I'll have *quality* . . . they marshall their *franchises very* carefull. Forty-two miles to Brandenburg the closest they could have another is here. I've got no competition. I'll have them coming in from Worth, from *Peacham* . . .

B. And it's just the down-payment . . .

A. What it is, yes, it's a down-payment, it's an *investment*, you're actually buying stock. Whatever it is, I looked it up a week ago. A couple of weeks ago, seventeen dollars a share. What is that? Two into thirty five, two shares for thirty-five, two hundred shares, thirty-five hundred dollars. Which you earn the dividend on, too, whatever that is . . .

B. on the stock.

A. Yes.

B. You should go with them.

A. I *would*. I *would* and I think I will. I think, June and I have almost decided to *go* with them. It's a big step, but I think it's worth it. That's what I think. Many things. You have to look down the road. It's a big step now, it's a big *investment*, it's a *commitment*, in certain ways it would mean taking on more *stock* . . .

B. Why is that?

A. Well, you have a basic *order*. Whatever your *size* is: the classification that they give you . . . on your *footage* . . . on your *overhead* . . . then when you order you have a minimum order that you have to file. (*pause*) You also have a minimum order per *month* . . . they come in and they do the inventory . . .

B. *They* do.

A. Yep. They do. At the end of the year . . . I think that that's a good idea. They come in, a team, ten people, something, calculators they're out in an afternoon, they come in Sunday afternoon . . . whenever you're closed, they work through the night, they're out Monday morning. *That's* a good idea . . . you ever do an inventory?

B. No.

A. Hell on Earth. I worked in a shoestore once. I thought I was going to go mad . . . But it's a big step. (*pause*)

B. Mm.

A. (*pause*) It's a big step. (*pause*)

B. *Well.* —

A. Yeaaah! Five of the Number 3. Twelve Inch. I'm almost sure I'll have them Friday.

B. I'll be back.

A. I'm going to call him again today. I would say ninety percent. Ninety-five percent. I'll have them Friday. I'll tell you: if he *doesn't* come in, I'm going to be down in Worth, Friday night, if he *doesn't* come in, I'll pick them up, you stop in Saturday Morning . . .

B. *That's* okay . . .

A. No. I should *have* 'em. No trouble at all. You come in Friday, he hasn't stopped in I'll have 'em Saturday first thing.

B. That's alright.

A. No trouble at all. I'm sorry I don't *have* 'em. I *should*. It doesn't help *you* to tell you that the *man* didn't come in.

B. Well, *thank* you.

A. That's alright. You take care, now.

B. You, too.

A. It's nice talking to you.

Deer Dogs

CAST

LARRY .... W.H. Macy
BUNCHY............................ Colin Stinton

Stage Manager .... Charles Otte

This play was first produced in May 1984 at the Ensemble Studio Theatre, Curt Dempster, Artistic Director, David S. Rosenak, Managing Director.

Deer Dogs

*Two men, LARRY and BUNCHY, at a country store.
There are also a couple of onlookers.*

LARRY. Dog's running deer it should be shot.

BUNCHY. But who's to tell it's runnin deer? *Law* says
you see a dog in pursuit of a deer you can *shoot* him.
Who's to say it's . . . wait, wait, you take *Dave* here: keeps
his dog tied up. One day the dog, say Larry *Thompson's*
dog, is runnin by—*Dave's* dog gets loose . . . Larry's
dog's runnin deer. Someone sees it and, down the road
later on, Larry's dog *and* Dave's dog. What does he do?
Shoot 'em both.

LARRY. How did Dave's dog get loose?

BUNCHY. . . . I'm saying a dog which is *usually* tied
down, *Dave's* dog . . .

LARRY. How did it get loose?

BUNCHY. I'm saying one day when it *is* loose . . . I
don't *know* how it got loose . . .

LARRY. And was it runnin deer. . . ?

BUNCHY. No.

LARRY. How do you know?

BUNCHY. Cause it hasn't got a *taste* for them. It's a
tame dog.

LARRY. How do you know?

BUNCHY. Well, now, now, now, because it *is* a tame
dog: I, you *know* that dog . . .

LARRY. . . . I'm . . .

BUNCHY. . . . *I* know what you're . . .

LARRY. I'm . . .

BUNCHY. I know what you're, wait a second—I know
what you're saying . . . that the dog is, *though* the dog is
tame, it gets loose it starts runnin deer. Is that it?

LARRY. Yes.

BUNCHY. But what I'm saying, this case we *know* that the dog is tame. It's *tame*. It *isn't* runnin deer. Alright? It's *DAVE'S DOG*. It's *tame*. It's been tied up constantly . . .

LARRY. How does it . . .

BUNCHY. . . . that's not . . .

LARRY. . . . how does it get loose?

BUNCHY. Well, say that Dave forgot to tie it up.

LARRY. And where does it go?

BUNCHY. . . .I . . .

LARRY. Where does it go?

BUNCHY. I know what you're saying. It goes to the woods. Alright.

LARRY. What is it doing there?

BUNCHY. It's *out*. With Larry Thompson's dog.

LARRY. What are they doing?

BUNCHY. *Larry's* dog is runnin deer.

LARRY. And what is Dave's dog doing?

BUNCHY. I don't know.

LARRY. Well, I don't know *either* — But I'*m* going to assume it's runnin deer. (*pause*)

BUNCHY. Would you shoot it?

LARRY. Yes, I would.

BUNCHY. You'd shoot Dave's dog.

LARRY. Yes. I would. (*pause*)

BUNCHY. (*snorts*) You would shoot Dave's dog. (*pause*)

LARRY. Yes. I would.

BUNCHY. Because you know that *that's* the dog that'll be caught. Not Larry *Thompson's* dog. (*pause*) *That's* the dog that will be caught . . . *Shoot*. It's a bad law . . . I'm sorry. (*pause*) I don't like it.

LARRY. You'll like it when you go out in the woods there ain't no *deer* . . .

BUNCHY. (*pause*) *Nossir.* (*pause*) No *sir* . . . N'I'm going to tell you one more thing: What the *Law* . . . wait a second—what the law *encourages* a fella to do is—I'm not saying *you* or *me*, but what it sets a man up to do is to say "I'm going to shoot that fella's *dog*." That's not right. (*pause*)

Columbus Avenue

For N. and F. Freund

Columbus Avenue

I felt the cold steel of a gun against my head three times.

Twenty six years we have been here. A tailor fourteen years before that here. Fifty-one years.

And he's an Orthodox Jew, and his father said (when he was managing; when first we settled on a price; and, you know, we *negociated* . . . but when we were done he told me:) "I will never throw you out."

The boy, he said, "Before I do a thing we'll talk." Today I get his letter in the mail. And I go there. I say, "You said that we were going to talk". He said, "I thought instead of talking I'd send you a letter."

So what am I going to do? Where am I going to go?

My customers are going to follow me? Can I ask them to walk for twenty blocks?

If even he gave me a *ten* year lease at least then I could sell the business.

So I said *double* the rent. *Triple* the rent, I told him.

He has got a *guy* is going to pay two thousand a month, he says. *And* he's going to put in fifty thousand dollars restoration.

I told him, "How is he going to make the *rent*?"

He said, "He'll break his back. He'll break his back the first year" (He didn't say 'back.'), "and, after that, he *fails*, I've got his fifty thousand he put in my building, and I rent the place again."

It's like that the whole street: things you don't want at what you can't afford, and nothing that you need.

No services.

Where am I going to go?

If I was twenty, if I was even ten years *younger* . . .

Where am I going to go? I got to move the *press*, I got

to move the *racks*; by the time I put *in* I put in all my savings to the *business* to go somewhere else and I have nothing. And I have to start again. Twenty-six years.

I told him, "I hate to remind you what your *father* said." He shrugged.

My *wife* went. I was getting sick. He said he'd give us an extension for six months.

It's the same all the neighborhood.

Let the depression come, and see who pays the rent.

Twenty-six years I've been here, and there are no more services on this street anymore.

What will people do I don't know what he thinks.

I don't know.

I don't know what I can say.

Two Scenes

Two Scenes

A. Give me a one.
B. Here is a one.
A. Give me a two.
B. Here is two.
A. Give me three.
B. I don't have three.
A. Give me a two.
B. Here is two.
A. Give me a one.
B. Here is one.
A. Give me a four.
B. I have four.
A. Give me a five.
B. Here is a five.
A. Give me a six.
B. Six.
A. Give me seven.
B. Yes.
A. Eight.
B. Yes.
A. Give me nine.
B. I don't have nine.
A. Give me eight.
B. Yes.
A. Give me another eight.
B. Eight.
A. Give me ten.
B. Here is ten.
A. Let me have ten again.
B. Ten.
A. Give me twelve.

B. Here is twelve.

A. Nine through twelve.

B. Yes.

A. Eight.

B. Yes.

A. . . . that was eight through twelve?

B. It was. We don't have nine. I mean "ten through twelve."

A. Yes.

B. . . . or "nine through twelve", but we don't have nine.

A. Yes. Give me eight.

B. Eight again?

A. Yes.

B. Here is eight.

A. And give me five.

B. Five.

A. One through three.

B. Yes.

A. No. *Three*. Is that right?

B. That is right.

A. Two alone.

B. Two.

A. Five.

B. Five.

A. Fifteen.

B. Yes.

A. Eleven.

B. Yes.

A. Eleven and five.

B. Yes.

A. *Two* eleven and five.

B. Yes.

A. *Three* eleven and five. Make that four . . . scrub that. Forget that. Give me six.

B. Six.

A. Six and five.

B. Go.

A. Six two five and five.

B. Yes.

A. One.

B. Yes.

A. Good. That's alright.

B. Are you done?

A. I think so. Yes. Thank you. Um, um, um. No. I think that's it. I'm done. Thank you. I'm finished. Fine. That's fine. That's very good; in fact I'm happy with it. (*pause*) That's very good.

SCENE TWO

SPEAKER.
Up. Everyone up. *Up* . . .
That's right.
Down slowly.
Down.
Now left. Left. Left.
And left.
Now right. *Hold* . . . hold it . . . up . . .
now center . . . left. Left Left.
Now down. Now left again and hold.
Return.
Now down.
Now up again. Now hold
And right right right

Now down and *hold*
Now cross
And back again.
Now *cross* . . .
Now *center* . . . *out* . . . and *hold it* . . .
out again . . . wait for it . . . out . . .
and *Good*!
(*pause*)
In. Now hold/ And *left*. Now hold.
And *in* now hold. And *right* now hold.
And *in* now hold. And *left* now hold . . .
and *in* now hold and *yes* and *out* and
left now hold and *down*.
(*pause*)
Good.
(*pause*)
Good.
(*pause*)
Very good.
(*pause*)
Wait. (*pause*) Wait. (*pause*) *Down* . . . (*pause*)
Down . . . (*pause*) *Good*! (*pause*) Good. (*pause*)
Good.

Conversations with
the Spirit World

CAST

MORRIS .... Frank Hamilton
JAMES .... Colin Stinton

This play was first produced in May 1984 at the Ensemble Studio Theatre, Curt Dempster, Artistic Director, David S. Rosenak, Managing Director.

Conversations with the Spirit World

Two Men

MORRIS. Dowsing for the like the kid says, "What cha doin'?" Says, "I'm *dowsing*." "What is that?" "I'm looking for this *line* . . ." "Line is *that*?" . . . "Line I'm *looking* for . . ." He points. "That *purple* line. . . ?"

JAMES. No . . .

MORRIS. *Yes*, and by dajn if he didn't point it *out*.

JAMES. He *saw* it. . . ?

MORRIS. Well, that's what I'm *telling* you . . . "What are you doing?" "Dowsing for a *well* . . ." By god, I'm trine to get these silly *sticks* to work . . .

JAMES. . . . uh huh . . .

MORRIS. S'i find this *line*, I'm trying to feel the line and Clark can *see* . . . I'll tell you something else: *Ivers*

JAMES. Now who is that. . . ?

MORRIS. Say Eighteen *thirty.* . . , say Eighteen, to Eighteen forty *five*, *fifty*, *hired* man up to Hayes place . . .

JAMES. Uh huh . . .

MORRIS. . . . he died, *Clara* said that he didn't go *over.*

JAMES. . . . old *Hayes* farm . . .

MORRIS. The Old *Hayes* Farm. The *Hire*d man. Now: Annie, she was *young*, you know, we'd hear her *talking* . . .

JAMES. . . . uh huh . . .

MORRIS. . . . young folks do, a little kid, you know, a year old, she'd be *talking* . . .

JAMES. She'd be talking to herself . . .

MORRIS. Uh huh . . . one day, we're up there, Clara asks her who she's *talking* to. She says, "This man . . ."

JAMES. Uh huh.

MORRIS. So she . . . now, I think, *I think* what Annie says is *Clara* asks her "What's his *name*?" Annie says "Ivan", something like that. Later it occurs to me, now where'd she get *that* from. . . ?

JAMES. The Russians.

MORRIS. . . . what *I* thought. But even *so*, something she *heard*? Where would she *hear* that. I told . . . I remember this, I'm telling stories on my *kids* . . .

JAMES. . . . uh huh . . .

MORRIS. To *Chunk*, I think it was . . .

JAMES. Chunk *Kellog*.

MORRIS. Yes. Said "Where she *gets* it from . . . some man named *Ivan*." He said, "Ask her was it Ivan she said or *Ivers*." Who he was, as I said, a *hired* man, hundred *years* ago.

JAMES. He die a violent death?

MORRIS. I don't *know*. What *Chunk* said . . . *yes*. Yes., I think he did. He, what *Chunk* said, he didn't want to go *across* . . .

JAMES. Uh huh . . .

MORRIS. And, to that *time* he habited the house.

JAMES. Annie remember this?

MORRIS. Well, you don't *know* . . .

JAMES. Uh huh . . .

MORRIS. Whether she, what she *saw*, or the *stories* . . .

JAMES. . . . uh huh . . .

MORRIS. . . . you know . . .

JAMES. Yes.

MORRIS. . . . that she remembers that we'd tell. And she *described* him.

JAMES. What'd she say?

MORRIS. A *man*, you know, I don't remember . . . *beard*.

JAMES. . . . uh huh . . .

MORRIS. A heavy *shirt* . . .

JAMES. Mm. (*pause*)

MORRIS. Reason *I thought* of it, dowsing for water, and *Clark* says/. . .

JAMES. Well, they say ninety percent *anyone* can dowse . . .

MORRIS. . . . that's right . . .

JAMES. . . . and a *hundred* percent all *children*.

MORRIS. That's right. (*pause*) That's right.

JAMES. *Jean* saw something out on the hill.

MORRIS. What was that?

JAMES. . . . the old *sugar* lane . . .

MORRIS. Uh huh . . .

JAMES. *Dusk* one day . . .

MORRIS. When was this?

JAMES. Last fall.

MORRIS. Uh huh.

JAMES. She got me, I was in the *bedroom*, she comes in . . .

MORRIS. What was it. . . ?

JAMES. She says "A boy". (*pause*) A boy? "Out at the entrance to the *lane*." "Now, who would *that* be. . . ?" I could tell, it was *something* she saw. I said "A *deer*." "No". "Waal, you know, they put that white *tail* up . . ."

MORRIS. . . . uh huh . . .

JAMES. She says "No, No, It wasn't a *deer*. *(pause)* It was a *boy*." She said they *felt* something, you know, like you do . . .

MORRIS. Mm . . .

JAMES. . . . she looked *around* . . .

MORRIS. Where was she?

JAMES. On the porch . . .

MORRIS. Mm.

JAMES. There was a *boy*. He *saw* her, and he ran up the lane. (*pause*) Now: (*pause*) Where would he be *coming* from. . . ?

MORRIS. . . . I don't know.

JAMES. Well, I don't know *either*. Nothing up there, and what would he be *doing* up there. . . ? (*pause*)

MORRIS. Now when was this?

JAMES. Just at dusk. I said "You see funny things in that light." (*pause*) "Yes." She says. "I saw this plain as day, though, and it was a *boy*. He *saw* me, and he ran away."

MORRIS. Did she say what he was wearing?

JAMES. No, and I'll tell you, I didn't want to *press* her. (*pause*)

MORRIS. Uh huh.

JAMES. . . . cause she was growing frightened. (*pause*)

MORRIS. She'd *seen* something.

JAMES. Mm.

MORRIS. You know what it was?

JAMES. No, I don't. (*pause*) No.

MORRIS. Mm.

JAMES. I know there's places in the woods where I don't like to *go* . . .

MORRIS. Mm. (*pause*) There's places I don't like to go *either*. (*pause*)

JAMES. *You* don't . . .

MORRIS. (*pause*) No. (*pause*)

JAMES. Mm.

Maple Sugaring

Maple Sugaring

The sugar shack had light slanted through the vent in the roof, and white smoke billowed up.

Morris's father built the place in 1912, and Morris was stoking the fire up now with hardwood logs.

The sap was clearer than clean water and ran through the vat. There was a superfine white foam on it, and often Morris took a scoop and dipped it in the vat then let it drip to see the thickness of the sap.

His wife made lunch. There was Canadian beer and Swiss Cheese, hamburgers and cookies made with the syrup that we made yesterday. The coffeepot leaned up against the vat to keep it warm.

Everyone spoke in hushed tones. Susan had brought down her eight-month old baby, and its grandmother, Morris's wife, set up Susan's old crib in the sugar shack.

He was asleep in the crib and his grandmother was looking down at him. She said "You're not the first child to nap in that crib while we were sugaring."

Later in the woods Joe, Susan and I were carrying the sap in pails, and she carried the baby on her back, and when we stopped to rest she nursed the child.

By four o'clock my neck hurt and I was becoming dizzy. The day had turned cold and the sap had ceased to run. Susan went in to set up dinner, I was left with Joe. We gathered the last buckets and I longed to go to sleep.

In the sugar shack the benches were made of wood. There was a square door on a running track to the woodshed. The sun streamed through the large vent in the roof. The people talked in whispers. The steam rose. Joe's baby was asleep.

Morris and Joe

Morris and Joe

Morris said, "Joe, 'member when we saw the bear in the tree?"

Joe smiled. "Remember when the milk froze?"

They were sitting on the step. The step had been removed from the house so they could repair the sill. It was an old house and the roof had leaked; the water ran down the post and rotted the sill. When they started the job Joe poked his pocketknife into it. It went in all the way.

The step was granite. Five-by-three. The bulldozer moved it back from the house. One corner was chipped out where there had been a bootscraper. Some hunters broke it out the year before.

Morris said, "You were shakin', Joe." Joe said, "I wasn't shakin'. I was scared for *you.*"

"You *were*?"

"Yes. I know how *skit*tish you get in moments of stress."

"A*ha.*"

Joe passed his lunchbucket to Morris who took a doughnut from it.

They looked out at the woods.

"I wonder where he is." Morris said.

"Probably up to Canada". Joe said.

"You think so?"

"Yes."

"Scared him within an inch of his life", Morris said. "U *huh* . . ." Joe got up off the step."

"Where are you goin'?"

"I'm goin' to pee." Joe walked behind a stack of lumber. Morris said, "Yes*sir* I hope he's back to Canada!"

"And why is that?" Joe said.

"'Cause he comes down here once again he better shake with *fear*. Cause he knows in America — he threatens our estates — there's not a man jack isn't ready to shoot himself in the foot."

"Do you remember when the milk froze?" Joe said.

"*Yes*sir. Smack in the foot", Morris said.

"*Susan* reminded me of that", Joe said. "That time that Morris cleaned the tank out." Joe came back buttoning up his fly. "How lovely all the driveway looked covered in milk . . ."

"You want some coffee?" Morris said.

". . . and how proud we were to defend you", Joe said, "From all that pernicious talk that you were drunk."

"People can sure be thoughtless", Morris said.

"That is the truth."

"Take you and that *bear*, frinstance", Morris said. "No mercy to dumb animals; just a display of wrath, and one man hopping with a .22 Long in his foot.

"I only hit the boot", Joe said.

"You want another cup of coffee?"

"No thanks."

Morris stretched and stood up. He closed his lunchpail. "Yessir!"

"You want me to go back to those left joists this afternoon?" Joe said.

"How many more you got to do?"

"Just the two."

"Might as well go do 'em."

They stood for a moment and looked at the sky. Joe sighed. "He sure was pretty singing in that tree."

"Yes. He was", Morris said.

"Where do you think he is today?"

"I'm sure he's back in Canada."

Morris spat on the ground. "Yup", he said. "Yessir", Joe said. They went back into the house.

Steve McQueen

Steve McQueen

A monologue. The speaker is a man in his mid-to-late thirties.

. . . well, I'*m* from Hawaii—I met him when he was at the Kalona Mar, he was there two months. He wasn't well. You know. We'd *talk* . . . we got to talking motorcycles. He asked if he could borrow my . . . bike, I said of course. He got to taking it out every day. He was registered there as "McGuire". He was keeping a low profile, you know? But after a week or two, you know, I think that he was lonely. I'd see him around the pool. He must have seen me one morning coming to work on my bike, because he asked me about it: how was it *riding*, something; and we started talking about bikes. He had at that time over one hundred bikes in his collection . . . I don't know where they were . . . in the States. You know, THE GREAT ESCAPE . . . ? He did those stunts himself. You know where he jumps the Barb Wire? He did that himself—though it wasn't barb wire.

He found out that I was in to Martial Arts and we took to sparring. He was in great shape—even though his disease—he was strong as a horse at that time. A fifty, sixty-minute workout was nothing to him. I'll tell you something else is he would drink a case of beer a day. Twenty-four beers a day. Lowenbrau. I know because I used to bring them to him. And smoke like a chimney. I guess he was just one of those men who are blessed with a completely perfect constitution. Though he was in great pain. I know that he was.

Indians . . . Harleys . . . Nortons . . . he had all of them. Did you know on the old *Indian* the oil used to go through the frame? It flowed through the frame. You know the stunt on THE GREAT ESCAPE where they get the bike? The German motorcycle rider's coming down the road, they stretch a wire. . . ?

They had the greatest motorcycle rider in the world . . . *Rusty*, something . . . *Rusty* . . . they told him "Just drive down the road." They told him, "Be ready for anything." That's why it's so authentic. He runs into that wire. . .? *He* didn't know it was there. They did it in one take. (*pause*)

I met his son. (*pause*) At that time he was training as a flight instructor. I stayed at his house in Malibu. Three days.

Yes

Yes

Two Men

A. People don't know when they're well-off.

B. Now that's for sure.

A. That's for *goddamned* . . . what did you say? It *is* for sure. It's for god-*damned* sure. I swear to christ. I swear on the grave of my mother, may she roast in peace . . .

B. What did you say? "May she roast in peace"?

A. Did I say what?

B. You said your mother.

A. Yes?

B. May she . . . (*pause*)

A. May she what? (*pause*)

B. She's dead, right?

A. Is she dead?

B. Is she?

A. Is that what you're asking me? (*pause*) Is my mother dead?

B. Am I asking you that?

A. Are you?

B. Well, is she dead? I *assume* that . . . she's *dead*, right?

A. (*pause*) Yes. (*pause*) Yes. She *is*.

B. (*pause*) I, um . . .

A. You're "sorry"?

B. I am sor . . . of, yes, of, ab . . . did she . . . of *course* I'm . . . did she . . .

A. Did she die recently?

B. Yes.

A. Recently? Peaceably. . . ? I don't mean "peaceably" I mean *Peacefully* . . . peacefully. Yes. Recently. Yes. . . . I suppose they're the same thing. No

. . . of course . . . of *course* they're not. They're not the
. . . *yes.* She's *dead.* She's absolutely *dead.* How's *your*
mom? Fine, I hope.

B. She's dead.

A. How about that?

B. I'm not glad that she's dead.

A. Well, that makes you a loyal *son, doesn't* it?

B. I liked her.

A. I'm very sure you did. That's "fine". That's truly
"fine" of you. What was I saying? (*pause*) What was I
speaking of, if I may?

B. You mentioned your mother.

A. Yes. I did. I said . . . what did I say? People are
not well-off.

B. You said:

A. I spoke about my mother. *Thank* you.

B. . . . something . . .

A. . . . that's correct . . .

B. "My mother . . ."

A. "may she rest in hell" ra . . . ra . . . rrrra . . . raaa
. . . rrrr . . . "may she . . ." ", "may she *rot* in hell" may
she . . . (*pause*) What's the phrase? MAY SHE REST
IN PEACE! What's the phrase?

B. May she rest in peace.

A. What's the phrase? (*pause*) What's the phrase for
that? (*pause*)

B. That's it.

A. That's it?

B. Yes. (*pause*)

A. There's another one.

B. There is?

A. What is it?

B. I don't know.

A. . . . the *phrase* for it . . . *you* know what I . . .

(*pause*) I must be a deeply troubled man. (*pause*) So many things accept me.

    B. What are they?

    A. I mean "*accept*" me.

    B. What did you say? (*pause*)

    A. I said . . . (*pause*)

    B. You said that you must be . . .

    A. . . . I said that things *accept* me.

    B. What did you. . . ?

    A. I . . .

    B. . . . you said . . . (*pause*)

    A. . . . I . . . (*pause*) . . . I . . . (*pause*) . . . I . . .

Dowsing

CAST

A . . . . Frank Hamilton
B . . . . Joe Ponazecki

This play was first produced in May 1984 at the Ensemble Studio Theatre, Curt Dempster, Artistic Director, David S. Rosenak, Managing Director.

Dowsing

Two older men, in a Vermont country store.

A. Y*essuh*. Fella told me he said "I don't want no more of them *dowsers* in here." By garry, I said, he's got a thing or two to learn.

B. I *guess* . . .

A. I said to you, Jim, *you're* a Mason, I said you did something I don't like, "I don't want no more *Masons* in here . . .

B. No. Mason's supposed t'believe in Brotherhood.

A. Yes. But if I told *you* something you did, I'se going to, you know, take it *out* on . . .

B. Yuh.

A. . . . on other *Masons* . . .

B. Well, I'd say that's *foolish*.

A. . . . What *I'd* say.

B. You say he didn't want the *Dowsers*?

A. *Dowsers* were down to his place . . .

B. . . . uh huh . . .

A. Some woman called, she wanted to know was her *friend* there, he says, "she's your friend, you should *know* if she's here." She called the Chamber of *Commerce*, he gets this *complaint*, the fella calls him up he says "by garry, *keep* 'em!" Says he'll do without 'em. Big mistake. One week of the year that they're here, he's *booked*, you know, they come t'spend their *money* . . .

B. Uh huh . . .

A. *They* don't care it cost twenty-five dollars, thirty-five, they don't care, they're, you know . . .

B. Um hmm . . .

A. Well, they're on *vacation. Any* business you meet some you'd rather not *deal* with. I think he's a *fool*.

B. Now: (*pause*) When you say "dowsin'" — is that the same dowsin' that we use to do with a bent stick?

A. It is.

B. For *water*.

A. Well, they dowse for *water*, dowse for *oil* . . .

B. For *oil*. . . ?

A. For oil in the ground. Yessuh.

B. . . . that a fact . . .

A. It is. For . . . well, you know, they might, say, you know, if they wanted to lay out a *field*, what to put where.

B. . . . yuh . . .

A. . . . in wha corner of the *field* . . .

B. Uh huh . . .

A. They'd dowse for that.

B. And how'd they find it?

A. Little *string*, *aweight* on it, they dowse it, yes or no. (*pause*) Eh? They ask the *question*, string moves *one* way, then it's "yes". The other way is "no".

B. The way it *rotates*.

A. *Yessir*.

B. You know, I could never . . . fellas take that *stick* . . . you know, I took it, never did a thing, just laid there in my hand. Other man took it, twisted every *which* way . . .

A. I know.

B. Never did a *thing* for me.

A. Me, either. (*pause*)

B. And that is their *convention*. Is that the thing?

A. Yup. Up *Morristown*. *You* know that.

B. Yup.

A. Yuh.

B. Up to *Morristown*.

A. Yuh. (*pause*)

B. I heard it's going to frost tonight.

A. They had a fellow, Connie *Barr* . . .

B. Yuh.

A. You remember Connie?

B. Yes, I do.

A. His sister lost her watch, he found it with a dowsing stick.

B. Who was his sister?

A. Eunice Craft/

B. The *Craft* girls. . . ?

A. No. She married Billy Craft.

B. She *married* Billy.

A. Yessir/

B. D'I know her?

A. I think you did.

B. Mm.

A. Lost her watch, he found it.

B. With a dowsing stick?

A. Uh huh.

B. Where was it?

A. In the field.

B. In plain sight?

A. I don't *think* so. Cause she'd lost it for a month.

B. She had?

A. Yeh.

B. And he found it?

A. Yes. He did.

B. Most like he *put* it there.

A. Well, that's what we thought at the *time*, but he held out he found it dowsing.

B. How about that now.

A. And I think that he *did*.

B. Well, you know, the things that you *see*, it makes you think that maybe there's something to *everything*.

A. Now, by God, that's the truth.
B. Mm?
A. *Yessir.*
B. *Ayuh.*

In the Mall

In the Hall

In the Mall

SCENE: *a bench in a shopping mall.*
CHARACTERS: *A — A sixty-year-old man.*
B — A thirteen-year-old boy.

B. I bet I know where you got that ice cream cone.

A. Where?

B. Down the mall.

A. That's right.

B. What did you pay for it?

A. Eighty-five cents.

B. Eighty-five cents . . .

A. That's right.

B. Is that with the tax/?

A. No.

B. What is it with the tax?

A. Eighty-nine.

B. Eighty-nine. That's right. I bought one there. (*pause*) I bought one there yesterday. What kind is it?

A. What kind is it?

B. Yes.

A. Butternut.

B. Butternut. I had one. (*pause*) They made it up. They made it up I went down there the guys in there, you know, down the mall, I don't know, they want everything just like they like it, you know what I mean? I went in there my shirt off, this guy he says "get out". (*pause*) I had to go. He was bigger than me — I would of wanted to smash his face in. Lots of people in there. They got a sign "No Shoes, No Shirt, No Service", all they care, who they *like*. Somebody they *like* goes in there they give 'em anything he wants.

I bought these crackers in a store they were crushed I took 'em back the guy said "you ate some of 'em". I said

I opened the box and I had a couple. "Eat the rest", he said.

I knew a fella had a dog he fed it scraps. Whatever he didn't want to eat. When he had his dinner. They got that same hat down there. Where did you get that hat? (*pause*) Where did you get that hat? Down there?

A. No.

B. Where did you get it?

A. I bought it on a trip.

B. They've got the same one down there. I like to know that. I saw a picture of this guy in there he looked like somebody I know. (*pause*) You think it's cold here?

A. No.

B. You don't?

A. No. (*long pause*)

B. Do you think it's warm? (*pause*)

A. No.

B. Well, if you don't think it's cold and it's not warm what is it? (*pause*) What *is* it?

A. What is it here?

B. *Yeah. Huh???* I don't think it's cold. I don't *care* if it's cold. *Anyway.* I like to do things, you know, that people say that they can't do. I climbed this fence once that everyone said you can't get over. It had barbwire at the top. They make this stuff it's razors. It's a razor-ribbon you can't climb it. I went up. You hold on to the barb wire you go right over I came down on the other side. *They* didn't care. They said that it was stupid. I bought a pair of socks once they had stripes on top I folded 'em down. I thought "maybe this is to show us where to fold." (*A gets up.*) Where are you going?

A. Home.

B. Why?

A. Why?

B. Yeah.

A. Because I'm finished here.

B. You're finished doing what?

A. Sitting here.

B. You are?

A. Yes.

B. Do you have any money? (*pause*) I need some cause I've got to do things.

A. No. I don't have any.

B. You don't.

A. No.

B. Mm. Mm. Mm. Mm. (*pause*) Do you throw that thing away when you're done?

A. Yes.

B. Mm. Where?

A. In the wastebasket.

B. Mm. (*pause*) Mm. (*A exits; pause.*) I had one one time . . .

Yes but so What

Yes but so What

Two Men.

A. She lost a tack I said "Well take your shoes off . . ."
Hey? ". . . you'll find it in one second."

B. . . . bitch

A. . . . man, all day long . . .

B. What did she need it for?

A. The fuck *I* know, when I come home . . .

B. . . . *hunh* . . .

A. . . . sit around all day . . .

B. . . . and then her *Father* died . . .

A. It's not her father, man . . .

B. . . . no?

A. It's not.

B. Who, I mean, it was, was it, who was it?

A. It was her father's *brother* . . .

B. . . . *what* is that. . . ? Her . . .

A. *No.*

B. How come? It's not her, *what*. . . ?

A. Her *uncle.*

B. Yeah.

A. It's *not* that, he was *step*, some thing . . . she *called*
him, she told you her *father* died?

B. I think I heard that wrong.

A. She *called* him Uncle. Uncle *Charlie* some like
that . . .

B. Her *uncle* . . .

A. What excuse is that. . . ? "Who broke the plate. . . ?"
"The *girl* broke it."

B. What plate. . . ?

A. Some . . . I don't know . . . "Ask the *girl*", Hey,
fuck, I'm gone out to ask the girl "Yes meester", all that
shit . . .

115

B. What is she?

A. Some, I don't know . . . from *Colombia*, some where . . .

B. What was the plate?

A. The plate? That my grandmother . . . *you've* seen it.

B. A blue . . .

A. No.

B. On the wall?

A. Up on the wall. Yeah. *Hanging* there . . .

B. Uh huh.

A. I come in, on the wall, "What *is* that. . . ?" *Knick* knacks . . . "Where's the plate. . . ?" "The girl broke it", Hey, I don't give a fuck. Don't laze *around* all day. Don't with your *t.v.* show, then lay this copping, copping, this, uh, copping *out* on me. *Tell* me. That's what I would ask. "Well, I dropped the *tack* . . ." Well *find* it. Huh? Unless what does this *indicate* when I come home? *I* don't know . . . something. *Huh*?

B. Yeah.

A. What?

B. I don't know.

A. Some, some, she's dis*sat*isfied. *Some* thing. Some *deep* . . . but, . . . Or let me try *this* on you: Broad in the bar:

B. Which one?

A. The looked-like-some . . . amateur *dike* alright? The no-tits ten years old, the *broad* alright?

B. You like that *young* . . .

A. . . . she wasn't that young, what I'm saying what she *looked*: some broads, I've *thought* this, I've sus*pec*ted this, you tell me I'm insane, I'm lookin' this broad in the bar . . .

B. . . . the *willow* broad . . .

A. Yes. What do you. . . ?

B. I don't mean "willow". What do I mean?

A. I don't know.

B. That *color* . . .

A. I don't know . . .

B. that . . .

A. What does it look like?

B. Like *yellow*.

A. I don't know. That she had *on*?

β. Yeah.

A. That she had *on*, or like in her *hair*?

B. That she had on. I *told* you . . .

A. On her *shirt*. . . .?

B. *Yeah.*

A. The broad with the yellow *shirt.*

B. Yeah.

A. In the *bar.*

B. Yeah.

A. She looked like a *dike.*

B. The young dike . . .

A. Yeah.

B. Yes.

A. What about her?

B. That's the *one.*

A. Yeah. (*pause*) Yeah. (*pause*) Hey. That's *her* problem. (*pause*) No, that's *her* problem. D'I tell you when I went home I saw a traffic accident?

B. No.

A. Yes. I did.

B. Where?

A. Eighteenth Street.

B. When?

A. Last night.

B. When we left the bar?

A. Yes.

B. What happened?

A. Some fucker got knocked down.

B. Was he dead?

A. No. (*pause*)

B. No? (*pause*)

A. He was moving.

B. He was?

A. Yeah. (*pause*) They had a lot of cars. (*pause*) Um. They had an ambulance. (*pause*) You ever think that will happen to you?

B. No. (*pause*)

A. I do sometimes. (*pause*) What I'm saying that the *thoughts* that you have. (*pause*)

B. Huh.

A. Do you know what I mean? (*pause*) That the *thoughts* you have will, um, they'll, that that they come *back* to you. (*pause*)

B. . . . uh . . .

A. That if you're *looking* at this poor man's got his *legs* chopped off with *glee*, some fuckin' thing, "How *happy* that I am. . . !", "that I'm alive," so on, or "that poor sucker with no legs . . .", that will come back to you. To *haunt* you. Time in, um, where was it . . . Newton, there was this, I knew this girl, she said that if you *do* a thing, you come *back*—I don't know if she believed that you *come* back, but if you *did*—you come back in the afterlife, you *are* that thing you scorned.

B. Like what?

A. Some sucker that you scorn. (*pause*) Like you make fun of a man, a *beggar*. (*pause*)

B. Huh . . .

A. *I* don't know. I think that thoughts transmit themselves. (*pause*) *I* don't know. But I think they do. They could . . . we never know the, look at *medicine*, one year "Do this . . ." The next year "We have this *discovery*, don't do *this* go do *that*." Or "All the shit that your *grandparents* did is right, we just found out. Because the blah blah blah and *science*." (*pause*) But they were stupid anyway . . ."

B. They could transmit themselves.

A. *Thoughts*?

B. Yes.

A. I know that. Tell that to me when I come home, because I'm thinking of this *broad*, alright . . . the . . .

B. Yeah.

A. The *dike* broad . . .

B. . . . with the ass . . .

A. That's right, and I come . . . not, not *even* when I come, *before* I have come in the door, alright? With, if I, I don't know that I *did*, but *if* . . . *if* I did, if I had let's, let's say if I'm coming in with *hostility* because of, that would be. If I had a *desire*, alright, and I come home, and *she's* . . . I'm saying: "I wish I was going home with *this* broad. *That* would make me happy. I swear to God that it would. (*pause*) It would be a simple answer to a lot of things and hurt no one." I come in the door, and I think "What's *stopping* me?", the fact I'm going home to someone . . .

B. . . . someone *else* . . .

A. My wife yes, and she's on the ladder with the lamp. I don't mean the lamp. With the *plate* . . . I don't mean the plate. Having *dropped* the plate. "The girl, your *plate* is smashed." What smashed the plate? (*pause*) My *hostility*. I'm not sain that it did. I'm not sain it did *not* . . . But what I am *saying* is *I Don't Know*. (*pause*) That . . . (*pause*) That . . . (*pause*) That . . . I think that *many* of us, alright, *much* of the time, I may be, I, I may be, maybe I'm full, maybe, what the hell, we all have the right to be wrong. Maybe, I'm, uh, maybe . . .

B. If we . . .

A. . . . hold on:

B. . . . if we . . .

A. Hold on:

B. If we weren't . . .

A. Yeah, yeah, yeah . . . if we *weren't* wrong . . .

B. . . . if . . .

A. If we *weren't* wrong . . .

B. The sci . . .

A. Yes. The scien*tif*ic things. Yes.

B. All the, yes.

A. That's what I'm saying . . .

B. The . . .

A. . . . the . . .

B. The in*vent*ions.

A. The in*vent*ions. Yes.

B. That . . .

A. *Yes.*

B. That were dis . . .

A. Yes. I'm saying, alright. Yes . . . Maybe I'm *wrong* . . .

B. . . . all that were discovered by . . .

A. Well, then that fucking proves my *point*, so shut . . .

B. That, um . . .

A. Alright. Alright, that's what I'm saying. (*pause*) Maybe I'm, *here*, in *this*, maybe I'm *wrong*. (*pause*) Maybe I am. That's what I'm saying.

B. They discovered them by chance.

A. I know they did.

B. Through being wrong.

A. Well, not through being wrong exactly, no, but other people *thought* they were. (*pause*) Is that what you meant? (*pause*)

B. Yes.

A. (*pause*) They *themselves* were wrong. Do you know why?

B. Because they didn't take the time to . . .

A. Ab . . .

B. To . . .

A. Absolou . . .

B. I don't mean "time . . ."

A. No, I know what you mean.

B. "care"

A. The *care* to . . .

B. Yes.

A. . . . That they didn't *trust* themselves.

B. They didn't *trust* themselves.

A. That's absolutely right.

B. To *see* . . .

A. To see the things before their nose. Or, wait a second here, to trust an *inner* . . .

B. Mmm.

A. To an *inner* truth . . .

B. . . . that they had seen . . .

A. Eh?

B. Yes.

A. An *inner* truth. (*pause*)

B. Yes.

A. Or a "*feeling*". (*pause*) What *are* feelings. . . ? *We* don't know what they are . . .

B. No.

A. We "feel" them . . .

B. Huh . . .

A. Big fuckin deal . . .

B. Yeah.

A. You know. . . ?

B. Like *sicknesses* . . .

A. Who *knows* what they are. . . ?

B. *No* one . . .

A. Just because we *say* . . .

B. . . . that's right . . .

A. We put a *name* on . . .

B. . . . yeah. We put a name on it, it makes us comfortable . . .

A. That's absolutely right.

B. What does it "mean". . . ?

A. *Bullshit* . . .

B. That's absolute . . .

A. It *doesn't* mean that we know what it is.

B. No.

A. *Bullshit. Bullshit. That's* all that it means.

B. Yes.

A. *Plants* . . . (*pause*) *Plants* or *flowers* . . . (*pause*) or *animals* or *thoughts.* Or *words* . . . what are *words*? *Words* for things, for things themselves . . . *bullshit* for *feelings* about things.

B. You're . . .

A. They stand in the *way.*

B. They *do.*

A. Of seeing what they are.

B. They do.

A. They're *such* bullshit . . .

B. They are . . .

A. . . . "*feelings* . . ."

B. . . . shit . . . (*pause*)

A. *Such* shit. *Such* nonsense. (*pause*)

B. You have to have the power to let *go.*

A. You *do.*

B. To go *beyond* . . .

A. To go, that's absolu . . . that's absolutely *right.* That's absolutely right. (*pause*) Something that we *say* . . . we put a *name* on it, and . . . (*pause*) and . . . (*pause*) and . . . (*pause*)

B. . . . like a *bowling* pencil . . .

A. I was thinking, that you're walking down the street, you have a *wrapper* of some thing. You say "I know what I should do. I know that I should throw it in the can." So you walk toward the can. You're tossing it, alright, the while you are you're knowing that it, I'm sorry, but it's true, while you are, you know that it won't go in. You, God knows why you do it, but you, huh, as if you're playing a *joke* on yourself. One part of your mind does not know what the other, huh. . . ? You toss it toward the can. You *know* it won't go in. It has no chance. You, *you* aren't going back. A part of you says "You knew that it wasn't going in the thing" . . . but you walk on. You say "What kind of a *world* is it when people like *me* can *do* things like that?" "I could have tossed it in the can." And you walk on. You think "I should be punished." As you cross the street you are hit by a cab.

B. Are you killed?

A. No. (*pause*)

B. Are you badly injured?

A. I think so. I don't know. Maybe. Maybe not, it's, well, to say you would, you would be crippled for life, on the one hand that seems harsh, you didn't throw the paper in the can. Eh? On the *other* hand, you are so, you know, who*ever*—I'm talking about, you know in your why go *separate* them? You know you are wrong. You've done a wrong thing. Maybe . . . may . . . (*pause*) maybe . . . (*pause*)

B. You want to know there is a God.

A. The guy, the wrapper.

B. That's . . .that's . . .

A. Why would you . . .

B. You want to know there is a . . .

A. Yeah, yeah, yeah. I *get* that, but why would you want to draw attention to him to yourself?

B. Behaving *badly*. (*pause*) You want to know there is a God, you miss the paper in the can, you don't go back. You're, um, you're *guilty*, *guilty*, right? You say: "The Blah Blah Blah, I'm going to roast in Hell". And yeah, yeah, so there is a God "These assholes on the, *they* don't know how bad I am . . . *God* does . . ." Why not to draw attention to your . . .

B. . . . yes . . .

A. By acting *good* . . . well, who *knows* what is good? We're assholes. (*pause*) I don't know . . . I don't know. I don't know *anything*. (*pause*) The fuckin *house* salad is no good; I'll tell you what I know: The, they call it "*House* salad", it's no good; a fellow, *and*, you take out a cigar, the *other* guy hands you one of his own says "Here . . ." alright?" Here, smoke a *good* cigar" . . . it is inv*ar*iably a piece of shit . . . (*pause*) What else? The broad says "I never *did* this before" is lying to herself. Those are the three things that I know.

B. Does she believe it?

A. The broad?

B. Yes.

A. There's something else that I know but I forgot what it is.

B. The broad . . .

A. "Does she believe it"? Yes. I told you. Yes.

B. Is it true?

A. No.

Cross Patch

"Cross Patch
Draw the latch
Sit by the fire and spin."
                    Mother Goose

Produced for the Atlantic Theatre Company by Sheila Welch and Larry Sloan.

CAST

M.C. . . . . W.H. Macy
ASSISTANT . . . . Steven Goldstein
PIERCE . . . . Colin Stinton
JOE BROWN . . . . Peter Riegert
QUESTIONER . . . . Clark Gregg
SLOAN . . . . Mike Nussbaum
CONVENTIONEERS . . . . . . The Atlantic Theatre Company

Stage Manager . . . . Felicity Huffman
Announcer . . . . Lionel Smith
Flute . . . . Karen Kohlhaas

Cross Patch

THE SCENE: *A meetinghall.*

THE CHARACTERS: *Speakers on the dais, members of the audience.*

MASTER OF CEREMONIES. . . . and of the European Section?

ASSISTANT. . . . ten.

M.C. . . . and of the Home Section?

ASSISTANT. Two.

M.C. Two of the Home?

ASSISTANT. Yes.

M.C. Two. Yes. Aaaaaaand . . . Thank you. (*He addresses the hall.*)

Our Friends. Of the Green Division. Thank you. I would like to introduce Doctor William J. Pierce, who is known to you.

A . . . who needs no introduction, but I will avail myself of the honor of giving him one. First in the hearts of all those who deeply love freedom — first in the fearful estimation of those who *oppose* it. You have seen him on this stage, and you have seen him in the Nation's Press. And in its consciousness. As he . . . throughout the Years since the Second . . . a veteran of three wars; holding the reserve, as you know, he . . . prefers to be addressed by his medical title . . . the reserve rank of Brigadier General in the Armed Forces of the United States. May we meditate on that for a brief instant, as he has said, from his, as I am sure you have read, "*Cross Patch* — the View of a Free Man," by William J. Pierce; which is, as he has said, why he prefers to present his public face as a *citizen*, rather than a soldier. A great soldier, who wrote: "Armed: what better word to signify

. . . a sense of pride, a sense of Honor, of our Sacred Charge—if we look to the Knights of Old, what did it signify? That one was *pledged to stand*—that, in assuming arms—we pledge ourselves accountable for our *acts*, for our *beliefs*, and *to* all those in our charge . . . to *stand* . . . 'till *death* . . . at our posts . . ."

"and what source of pride," he writes, ". . . it gave to me . . . in our posts through the years . . . numbering thirty years . . . to say, to paraphrase, to reverse that lovely phrase written to the Corinthians, to say: 'what I am with you frightens me, what I am *for* you comforts me.'" My friends: William J. Pierce.

(*The audience applauds. WILLIAM J. PIERCE moves to the podium.*)

PIERCE. Mr. Chairman. My friends. What must a man feel who has won the lottery?

In papers every day. You see a man . . . a *workingman*. Who's been awarded. Some gigantic sum. Millions of . . . This man's life is changed. To his wife, to his friends he says: "I'm as I was before—the thing which gave me pleasure still will do. Those things I cherish will not be affected by this great fortune . . ."

To himself he says, "How will I change? *Surely* this sign from God"—how can he see it otherwise? Singled from millions of men, his hope *alone* blest—surely he must, in his heart, see it as a proof of divine providence, of endorsement of that secret thought. (we all have had it) "I am *blessed*. I am a special man."

Let's stop a moment here. On one extreme you see this thought expressed in Messianic Dreams, dreams of the demagogue—illusions of grandeur . . .

And on the bottom of the scale we see those (and we

see them every day) oppressed, downtrodden, *devoid* of the most minimal modicum of Self-Esteem — slunk in the gutters, in the alleyways. Cowering in jobs they despise, weak, subservient, subserviated to their inability to *avow* their desires — to be Special. To be blest. To be *singled out for the good each of us knows is in his breast.*

And so we have two aberrations of the norm: delusions of Grandeur, and, on the other hand, a suicidal wish to be ignored, to be punished, for — finally — for harboring that same wish for a Divine Love.

The ordinary man — like ourselves, let us say, . . . one day content, the next day not; in some things talented, in some things dull; full of pride, full of hidden fears, feelings of . . . *Torn Every Day* between that part of him which says "there is a god — be humble, find a meaning in this life," and "go your way, get those things which can give you comfort, think of nothing, simply live and die."

This man, like you and me, when his most hidden wish is broadcast to the world, what does he do? When, yes, the heavy hand of providence taps him and says, "you are the one — among all — those who have watched and prayed — you are . . ." . . . and frees the man from want. And from material anxiety, and sets him . . . *as* a City on a Hill — To those in whose midst he happily toiled, and in whose happy midst he never will again . . . this man . . . abstracted from his home, translated to a pinnacle, assaulted by *greed* . . . *fear* . . . *greed* . . . *hatred* . . . *not* unlike the Christ, for was it his goodness they hated? *All* of them were good. They killed him for that he had been *preferred* . . . as that man who had won a contest and had wished to win. My parallel . . . (*pause*)

My friends. In this world. As molecules move, as

pigeons on the lawn move, as the stars in *their* predestined sway . . . so in the affairs of our so imperfect striving breed, so we are governed by forces we cannot see. Nor *ever* understand. Endorsed by Providence — why? What *course* shall we take? Our holy land? To, messianically proclaim, "yes. Yes. I am the . . . you have waited for the one!" Or, as the abject wretch say, "Forget me, I will not hear the call."

Our happy land.

What course shall we . . .

Blest by a Jealous God, or blest by Random Chance with Freedom. How shall we enjoy it? Freed from Fears . . .

Single out, yes. We must acknowledge it . . . our lives *have* changed.

The Signal of the World — that shining city . . . we can never shrink out of the world's gaze, or quiet that gaze through force. Where can we find humility? (*pause*) The force of arms. An armed man, blest by god, with the strength of *will* . . . That is, with . . . *not* blind to the essence of this life, which is, that it is fleeting. With the will to say: "not as a gambler, rather as a *priest* I consecrate those things . . ." Listen to me: ". . . not, not to my *possession* . . . given to my *charge* . . . as *steward* of this life . . . of those great gifts, of the Eternal gift of freedom . . .

I will *guard* that trust, as of another whom I love . . . *sans* bravery or show, or the desire of praise, but through my understanding of my place. Under God. With my fellow men. My blessing is a charge and my arms are a sign: (the bearing of arms) that I do *accept* that charge . . . as did the Knights of Old . . . I find that intersection of the pommel and the hilt *significant* . . . That cross . . . (*pause*) I will take it up. I will protect that which was given to my keeping . . . with my life. So help me God.

And so find happiness. Thank you. (*PIERCE sits amidst applause. The M.C. rises.*)

M.C. And now a . . . (*aside*) Did we do the. . . ?

ASSISTANT. (*aside*) Yes.

M.C. (*to the hall*) A Friend of our Friends, a friend of *ours*, and, *in* this time, a man who, as the Gen'ral said, is not afraid to make allegiance known: Joe Brown.

(*Amidst applause JOE BROWN goes to the podium, assembles his notes.*)

JOE. Thank you. Thank you all. Esteemed hosts, Brothers, Pals . . . I am reminded of a guy in Europe, a ballplayer as it happens. In the War, he's in Pigalle in Paris. He sees this hooker. A gorgeous . . . piece of ass . . . legs up to . . . *young*, alright? The . . . goes up to her —three words of French—he goes "Combien?" She answers him, this rapid stream, he don't know what she, "blagadelablahbegela . . ." He says "Lentement! Lentement!" . . . and she says "Oui!" But I'll try to be brief. 1919. Arnold Rothstein, "A.R." to his friends, Hotel Ansonia, New York. Dad was in, I believe, the Rag Trade . . . many of them *were* . . . son of a *devout* man, son . . . of course, a disappointment to him. Saw the movie? Bit the father says "kaddish," his son is dead? A dead son. Not that bad, but almost . . . (*pause*) A *multi* millionaire, I'm talking 1910, nineteen-fifteen, in there, no, or small income tax.

Here's the thing: *Comiskey*, as we know, perhaps the finest team ever seen in professional baseball; what's the average? Six, five or six thousand bucks a year he's paying to men who, they went *elsewhere* could start at three times that. Ballplayers getting twice that, mediocre men, easily, he's starving them.

Days of the Reserve Clause. Means you work for me or you don't work. Virtual indentureship. The men were riled. Eddie Cicotte, Shoeless Joe Jackson, legends in their time. Men up against the . . . wives, et cetera . . . *up* against the wall. National Pastime. On the one hand, everything for show, nothing for the . . . but nothing for the Boys. Team riled, unhappy . . . tried an abortive strike, which didn't . . . Rothstein comes to them. Our largest Gambler. "Put it in the Tank," he goes: "You lay down for the Cincinnati Reds . . ." (*Someone brings him water.*) Thank you . . . The . . . what is this?

WATERBEARER. Water.

JOE. Thank you. Rothstein. "You throw the Series and you'll never have to work ag . . ." (*drinks water*) Now. Okay. The time the Series comes about it's seven-to-five Sox, six-to-five and *pick* 'em, even money, seven-to-five Reds, *eight*-to-five Reds. The word is, Cincinnati players calling out the Sox: "Is it true that you threw the Game?" The rest is history. Now: whence this seemingly new concept of advocacy for athletes? You might say 1919, Blacksocks. You might say . . . in that same year, the Actors Union, faced with a . . . *another* strike. That same year. You . . . faced with a trans . . . faced with a transitional, I think we might say . . . between, on the one, concepts of *serfdom* . . . (let's not balk at . . .) the idea that a man may indenture others, may, in effect, own that work; and, on the other hand, let's say, a Socialist State eschewing property entire . . . where . . . the work of the individual . . . we understand . . . what have. . . ? What have we. . . ? Between the. . . ? Between the two: A Free Market. Which, al. . . ? redounds to the benefit of. . . ? Well: The Blacksocks said what? Abso. . . . ? Ridden by guilt, nonetheless . . .

The in . . . But could not: Chuck Comiskey (Field

bears his name today.) "I . . . I'm the owner. They belong to me. I'll pay 'em what I want. That's what I'll pay 'em." (*pause*)

What I would like you for *tomorrow* to: Rationalize the . . . so we do not say, because I know that this is . . . many of you do. Others have spoken here about avoiding zero-sum. "I win/you lose," strategic, though, in speaking for your man, from time to time, we *must* . . . aaaand, we know, from, as an *exercise*, your: *At* the strike, *during* the strike, given intransigent behavior on the owners . . . with *Rothstein*, and with the Grand Jury: to represent *cogently*, *concisely*, as *Churchill* said: "Muster your arguements upon one side of a sheet of paper." To determine. One: what it is that my client wants. And, again, to employ, as we heard yesterday, the Method of Parameter . . . Two: how do I Get It? Or, f'you will: tactics and strategy. Now: also: for each one of you . . . and I'd like a paper. . . :

During the strike, the proposed strike, and: after the *scandal*, to present and defend Comiskey's position as the owner of the club. (*A QUESTIONER on the floor raises his hand.*) Yes.

QUESTIONER. Was the club wholly owned?

JOE. Wholly owned by Comiskey. Yes. (*another QUESTIONER*)

QUESTIONER II. How long should the paper be?

JOE. You're representing a man. How long should your fight be? (*pause*) The Romans had a law, the name of which now escapes me, and you've heard of it before, that the test, the prime test of *negligence* in *agency* was this: put as a question to a reasonable man, eh? Did the Agent prosecute his client's interests *better* than he would have acted for his own. The name of that law was?

MAN IN HALL. Lex (TK).
JOE. Thank you. Mr. Sloan. . . ?

(*JOE retires to his seat, another man takes his place at the podium.*)

SLOAN. (*pause*) When we get home we will find things have changed. At once, at once things change and our *view* of them alters. So that a Static State is an illusion.

Many will say "where have you . . . where have you been?"

The rage that they feel at *not* having been there will express itself in . . . doomed to loneliness, then, many will deny the fact of love. If you will. In Australia we heard that returning troops, taunted with innuendos of our own men opened fire on them. Men from the Great War. Sitting in a garden, Years, or thought they did . . . remembering what? Our own George *Patton*, who slapped that Jewish Boy . . . your *wives* . . .

Your . . . on return, who would cry "Embrace Me." Or "Share your thoughts with me. Share . . . your innermost being."

In a happier time.

Governed by Code.

A man would compartmentalize his life. Now: in a world ruled by war. Vast and horrific weapons, they tell us, loom on the horizon. Huge bombs capable of destroying a City Block. We have seen gas, and the machine gun, and *tanks*. (*pause*) And armored . . . Once, arms swathed, a faceplate, young men fought for Honor. In the Dueling Schools, and, once, in Japan, where day and night, wrong and right, a man and his State, his God, his conscience were distinct . . . but not now. And when you go home you will find things have changed.

Be of good faith with your faith. Trust in God. The things which you see, which transpire, are *real*. Though they are frightening, and we may say that *you* are the apparition. As you are. Locked in a prison. Locked . . . one day as any day the concerns of that day obliterate . . . remember: at your death you will say *happiness* was just those days. Friendship, comradeship, comaraderie, love, competition . . . in an orderly . . . this saying: What is *constant* in the world? *I* am. (*A pause. He takes his seat. The M.C. stands behind the podium.*)

M.C. Thank you. (*pause*) Thank you. (*pause*) I think that's . . . oh! We have ann. . . ?

ASSISTANT. Yes.

M.C. We have announcements.

ASSISTANT. (*stands at his place*) Several of you have asked about the picnic. You are free to bring whomever you like. They need *not* . . .

M.C. . . . the price includes the . . .

ASSISTANT. . . . yes. The price is for you and a friend. You must . . .

M.C. . . . *any* friend, that would be . . .

ASSISTANT. . . . your *wife*, your *sweetheart*. A friend, an acquaintance, *any* . . . but you must, as there is the one ticket, you must present it *together*.

M.C. . . . at the . . .

ASSISTANT. . . . at . . .

M.C. . . . at the Gate.

ASSISTANT. At the gate. Yes.

M.C. Now: We:

ASSISTANT. One more.

M.C. I'm sorry.

ASSISTANT. We've been given an opportunity to buy . . . you saw the list on the board . . . many items of surplus from Bartell. He's giving us twenty-percent off—

the list price is on the board. You have 'til the first, and I *urge* you, if you've looked at the list, take advantage of this, it's a once-in-a-life-time offer.

(*From the floor.*)

QUESTIONER IV. What's on the list?

ASSISTANT. The whole "K" series.

QUESTIONER IV. And the "102"?

ASSISTANT. You'll have to check, but I believe it is. (*to M.C.*) Alright.

M.C. Did you. . . ?

ASSISTANT. Oh. (*pause; checks papers*) The family of John Murray . . . many of you knew John. John died in South America with the Green Division last month. (*pause*) Katy has asked that we, to those who knew him— we have a list of his personal effects . . . (*He refers to list.*) His battle ribbons, a . . . his zippo lighter with a crest of the One Hundred Ninth . . . His Browning Hi-Power . . . which I believe is the one which he carried in Africa. (*pause*) Many of you who knew him . . . (*pause*) Who . . . (*pause*) Well. The list is on the board, the items are for sale. The proceeds go to his family. Thank you. (*He sits.*)

M.C. To you all; *Thank* you all. For making this the success it has been. Let us say, as we always say:

Good Luck, Good Weather,

Bright at Dawn.

We step where those have stepped before.

A Happy Heart.

Strong shoulders to the wheel.

What is the password?

ALL. Answer to the Call.

M.C. What is the Call?

ALL. Willing to serve.

M.C. (*arranging his papers*) Until we meet again.

Goldberg Street

Produced by Sheila Welch and Larry Sloan for the Atlantic Theatre Company.

CAST

MAN .... Mike Nussbaum
DAUGHTER........................ Susan Nussbaum

Stage Manager .... Felicity Huffman
Announcer .... Lionel Smith
Flute .... Karen Kohlhaas
Press .... Boomer Boznos and Smokey Bandle

Goldberg Street

A man and his daughter talking.

MAN. Goldberg street. Because they didn't h*a*ve it. They had S*mith* street — They had *Rybka* street. There was no Goldberg street. You can keep your distance and it's fine. If a man is secluded then he feels superior. Or rage. But where's the good in that?

DAUGHTER. There is no good in it.

MAN. I'm not sure. And I'm not so sure. But sometimes . . . (*pause*) And sometimes, also — you must stand up for yourself. Because it is uncertain. . . . what we're doing here. And masses of *people* do now this and now that; and *at the moment* you might say "this seems wrong", or "this seems attractive" Popular delusions warp . . . you cannot say they are the product of one man. Some men like hunting. I enjoy it myself. Some men like to kill. Many have killed. Many would say this is not a bad thing. But they know it is. Which is not to say they have not enjoyed it.

A man would *wish* . . . (*pause*) A man would wish someone to inform him . . . I, if I may say, this is a good example — I am not mechanical but if something is broken and I *must* fix it there comes a point at which pride *in my*self — for the alternative is to say that I am not a man, or that I am an impotent or *stupid* . . . or, in some way unable to do those things many have done . . . At one point I would say: "It now is mine to fix it". When it's up to *me* — if there is no one there . . . then I *will* fix it — for it isn't hidden. So with problems . . . those things where one *cannot* refer to someone. At some point. One must say: *I* am the . . .

DAUGHTER. . . . the authority.

141

MAN. . . . the, *loneliness* that that entails, of course
. . . and who would be so drole as to form a religion on
ethical principles? (*pause*)

And one is alone.

And *so* one is . . .

And so what.

From *that* one may say "well, then I can proceed . . ."

Lost in the wood you must say "I am lost".

DAUGHTER. You killed the deer.

MAN. The man in *Bregny* . . . (*pause*)

Men hunted them with automatic weapons.

Which is not a sporting way and it is not an effective way.

Because you can't *aim* them, truly . . .

DAUGHTER. . . . because they jump.

MAN. They *do* jump. And . . . You can aim the first
shot, of course . . . But we were taught to fire them from
the hip. Held on the sling to give it tension.

And they *hunted* them, and, as you couldn't aim your
shot, the animal, hit badly . . .

Ran

Died.

Left a blood trail, but they couldn't follow it.

Or wouldn't.

Although they were country boys.

And, I'm sure . . . revered life.

Loved hunting . . .

. . . anyway.

(*pause*)

They couldn't read a compass.

In Arkansas one time we were lost. The leader asked
if anyone could read a compass. We'd all heard the lec-
ture. I said, well, I'd never *held* one, but I heard it, I
supposed I . . . took it. Read it. Followed the map. Led
up back to camp. It was easy enough. None of it was

difficult. And they put me in for the Unit. When they asked for volunteers. Which may have been a joke. It was a joke. For anti-semitism in the Army. Then. Even now . . . (*pause*)

Even for, and especially then which I see as . . . If you look at the world you have to laugh. They scorned me, as I assume they did, for those skills they desired to possess. And it was funny I had them. To them. Lost in the woods. It seems simple enough. If you just take away the thought someone's coming to help you. (*pause*)

DAUGHTER. You never see them?

MAN. No, although we were close. In a way. Over there. Where would we . . . I have no desire to go down south (*pause*) To go visiting at all.

DAUGHTER. You went to France.

MAN. I did. It was the Anniversary. I wanted to see.

DAUGHTER. What did you see? (*pause*)

MAN. People. (*pause*) I saw the Town.

DAUGHTER. Had it changed?

MAN. No. It hadn't changed. Just as the world has changed. (*pause*)

DAUGHTER. I heard they saw you.

MAN. Yes. They saw me. There's always someone there. Laying flowers — it's right by the Cliff. I mean the cliff is right beside the road. They . . . (*pause*)

DAUGHTER. They knew you.

MAN. I was . . . no, they didn't know me. They saw someone standing . . . (*pause*) A man spoke English. He went in the Pub. He must have said, he said something like "one of them's come back". And, in the cemetary . . . they came over there.

DAUGHTER. You were reading the stones?

MAN. They're crosses, really . . . (*pause*) Yes. I was looking for the names.

DAUGHTER. Did you find them?

MAN. I thought that I would not remember them. I . . . but I . . . (*pause*) People from the Pub came out. (*pause*) They said "you were here". Yes. We wept. Patton slapped that Jewish boy. They said . . . (*pause*)

DAUGHTER. They remembered you. (*pause*) They remembered what you'd done.

MAN. They sent me for a joke. Because I read the compass. I was glad to go. I knew they thought me ludicrous. Our shame is that we feel they're right. (*pause*) I . . . have no desire to go to Israle. (*pause*) But I went to France.